BETWEEN ONE FAITH
AND ANOTHER

Engaging Conversations on the World's Great Religions

PETER KREEFT

IVP Books

An imprint of InterVarsity Press
Downers Grove, Illinois

InterVarsity Press
P.O. Box 1400, Downers Grove, IL 60515-1426
ivpress.com
email@ivpress.com

InterVarsity Press® is the book-publishing division of InterVarsity Christian Fellowship/USA®, a movement of students and faculty active on campus at hundreds of universities, colleges, and schools of nursing in the United States of America, and a member movement of the International Fellowship of Evangelical Students. For information about local and regional activities, visit intervarsity.org.

Scripture quotations, unless otherwise noted, are from the New Revised Standard Version of the Bible, copyright 1989 by the Division of Christian Education of the National Council of the Churches of Christ in the USA. Used by permission. All rights reserved.

While any stories in this book are true, some names and identifying information may have been changed to protect the privacy of individuals.

Cover design: Faceout Studio
Interior design: Daniel van Loon
Image: © Lubushka/Thinkstock

ISBN 978-0-8308-4510-1 (print)
ISBN 978-0-8308-9084-2 (digital)

Printed in the United States of America ♾

g green **As a member of the Green Press Initiative, InterVarsity Press is committed to**
press protecting the environment and to the responsible use of natural resources.
INITIATIVE **To learn more, visit greenpressinitiative.org.**

Library of Congress Cataloging-in-Publication Data

A catalog record for this book is available from the Library of Congress.

P   25   24   23   22   21   20   19   18   17   16   15   14   13   12   11   10   9   8   7   6   5   4   3   2   1

Y   34   33   32   31   30   29   28   27   26   25   24   23   22   21   20   19   18   17

CONTENTS

INTRODUCTION

This book is about the second greatest conversation in the world. The greatest conversation in the world is the conversation between ourselves and God. The name for that is "religion." It means "relationship." The English word *religion* comes from the Latin word *religare*, which means, literally, a binding-back relationship.

The second greatest conversation in the world is the conversation among the different religions—that is, the different human conversationalists in the first and greatest conversation. The name for that is "comparative religions."

The first conversation is vertical. All religions converse with someone or something greater than ourselves. The second conversation is horizontal. One of the issues in that conversation is whether one religion is greater or truer or better than another. Are the different religions in the world incompatible or compatible?

There are three possible answers to this question. These answers are called by philosophers of religion "exclusivism," "inclusivism," and "pluralism."

Exclusivists say that the religions of the world contradict each other, at least in some essential points, so that some religions must be untrue in some essential points.

Inclusivism says that deep down, perhaps at some "mystical" level, religions do not contradict each other. In fact that they are really one, like apparently different islands united underwater (mystically) as parts of the same undersea mountain, or different roads up the same mountain, converging at the top.

Pluralism says we cannot know which it is. It is skeptical of both of the other two positions and says that we can only know that the religions of the world are different, like lions and tigers, and not whether they are compatible and marriageable into a "liger."

This book considers that question of comparative religions. It is also a very quick tour through the essential teachings of seven of the world's great religions to gather enough data for the three characters (and the reader) to form a reasonable opinion or theory of comparative religions, a theory that judges the data. The questions in these dialogues are motivated by an attempt to find that unfashionable thing called truth.

Truth is ultimately what God thinks. All truth is God's truth (as Wheaton College's Arthur Holmes famously said). So our attempts to find truth are ultimately attempts to read God's mind. Regarding the world, sometimes reading God's mind is easy $(2+2=4)$ and sometimes harder $(E=mc^2)$, but it is hardest of all concerning religions. Clearly the religions of the world are different, playing and singing different musics. The question of comparative religions is hardest of all because it is the question of how these different musics sound to God. Are they in harmony? Does one carry the lead? Are they in cacophony?

Spoiler alert: we are not God, therefore we will not find the final answer to the question of how the different religions sound to God. At least not in this life. So it is a wild goose chase. We will not catch the goose. But a wild goose chase is a very good thing to do anyway. And along the way we may find some very important answers to questions that are only a little bit less ambitious.

Dramatis Personae

Here are the characters in my little drama and their different methods of approach.

- Thomas Keptic, a hard-headed, logical, nonreligious *exclusivist* who uses the scientific method, treating ideas as false until proven true rather than vice versa. He uses the light of logic in a sincere search for truth, like an explorer of new continents.

- Bea ("Bee") Lever, an open-hearted, intuitive, religious *inclusivist* who uses the unscientific and personal method of treating religions as true until proven false. Like a bee, she is engaged in making honey from nectar gathered from many flowers.

- Professor Fesser, a neutral, scholarly, objective *pluralist* who uses the aesthetic or artistic method of listening to and looking at each different religious datum carefully before pronouncing on its value, truth, or compatibility with the rest of the data, like a listener at a symphony or a visitor to an art museum.

The three isms mean something different in this context—the study of comparative religions—than they do elsewhere. For instance, *pluralism* does not necessarily mean that a society with a plurality of different religions is inevitable or socially and politically preferable. *Exclusivism* does not necessarily mean that those who do not believe the one and only religion that is totally true cannot be saved. And *inclusivism* does not necessarily mean that religions are all the same, that there are no important differences. Pluralism claims that we do not know whether or not the religions of the world contradict each other. Exclusivism claims that they do. Inclusivism claims that they don't.

A Personal Note on Where I'm Coming From

This is a work of imaginative exploration, not apologetics. My own position does not exactly coincide with any one of these three characters, though I have deep sympathies for all three.

Thomas is an atheist, or at least a skeptical agnostic, and a rather negative and cynical one. I made my exclusivist character an atheist simply because atheists tend to be hard-headed, scientific, logical, and critical, not because all atheists are exclusivists (they're not) or because all exclusivists are atheists (they're not). In fact, most exclusivists are believers and most believers are or at least have been exclusivists. Most of the great theologians, saints, and religious philosophers of the past were exclusivists.

I made Bea an inclusivist not because all believers are inclusivists (they're not, though some are) but to show a triple difference between her and Thomas: heart versus head, believer versus unbeliever, and inclusivist versus exclusivist. No one of these three differences logically necessitates any of the other two. Bea can at times be naive, fuzzy thinking, and so open-minded that her brains seem to spill out; but she can also be very perceptive and profound. As Thomas is a logical, left-brain thinker, Bea is an intuitive, right-brain thinker.

Professor Fesser believes that a professor, unlike a preacher, ought to be detached, objective, and noncommittal, even though this makes him at times appear wishy-washy. But he is a good professor; and a good professor sometimes refuses to "profess" his own personal beliefs in class but performs as an actor playing a part (or playing two contrasting parts), so that students can look more clearly and fairly at the objective truth of the issues rather than at their professor's personal, subjective mind.

All three positions, and all three characters that espouse them, have problems and faults. I tried to make the characters real concrete persons, not abstractions, idealizations, or allegories.

I find all three of these fictional characters in myself, as parts of myself, and I empathize with all three: with Thomas's hard-headed logic, with Bea's open-hearted love of wisdom everywhere, and with the professor's fair and even-handed justice. I also find some important truth in all three answers to the question of comparative religions. In exclusivism because the theologies of different world religions do quite clearly appear to contradict each other. In inclusivism because the moralities and spiritualities of the world's great religions do really appear to profoundly agree about the most important questions, and the saints of different religions are strikingly similar, even when their beliefs are strikingly different. And in pluralism because religions do really appear to be as individual as people, with no one simple, objective, and neutral way to rank them.

So this book is not an argument for only one of these three positions and a refutation of the two others. It is an exploration on a path whose end I do not clearly see. (I find that writing books and teaching classes are surprisingly effective ways of teaching myself things I did not know before.) That is why this book is in the form of a dialogue—or trialogue—rather than a monologue, like most books. It is Socratic. It is a trialogue in the double sense of a three-part conversation and a "try," an "essaying," an exploration.

The characters are not good guys versus bad guys. There is no hero and no villain, no Socrates and no Sophist. Thomas is an atheist (as I am not) but he is honest and rational. Bea is an inclusivist (as I am not—I think) but she is a Christian (as am I). The professor is a pluralist (as I am not—I think) but he is fair and reasonable.

You don't have to agree with me or with any of the three inter-locutors to enjoy and profit from this book.

I think I should say more. I should give you a full disclosure here: exactly where am I coming from? What am I most certain about? About Christ. That is why I am an exclusivist. There is only one Christ, only one God incarnate. Yet the fact that this Christ enlightens everyone who comes into the world (John 1:9) opens the door to the possibility of a kind of inclusivism. But this inclusivism is not divinely revealed data but only a human interpretation of that data or a deduction from it. If inclusivism is true, it is like the doctrine of predestination and eternal security—true from the divine point of view, but probably not from the human. And I do not have the divine point of view. (You may quote me on that!) Christ, who does have the divine point of view, never answered the question of comparative religions.

So Christ is the only one I am certain about. In a lesser sense I am also certain of Socrates—that is, of three features of Socrates and the Socratic method: the need for the honest use of reason (which seems to lead to exclusivism), the need for intellectual humility (which seems to lead to pluralism), and the need for open-mindedness and maximally charitable interpretations (which seems to lead to inclusivism). The strongest argument, to my mind, for inclusivism is the character of God, which always sur-prises and amazes us and exceeds our expectations in mercy, love, and welcoming.

For a Christian, Christ cannot be half of the way, the truth, or the life: he is all of it. If he is not all, he is nothing, he is a fake. But Christ is a mystery. All the essential articles of the Christian faith are "mysteries." That was the word the early church fathers used for what we call doctrines or dogmas. And that word gives us a lot of room for speculation about issues not addressed clearly and explicitly by divine revelation, by the faith once and for all delivered to the saints. The issue of comparative religions is one of them.

By the way, I have received critical comments about my book *Between Allah and Jesus: What Christians Can Learn from Muslims* from both sides of the spectrum, from those who thought it too hard and those who thought it too soft; that is, from those who thought it too exclusivistic or "triumphalistic" and those who thought it too inclusivistic, too compromising and "ecumenical." This proves nothing, but it suggests that those who admire and try to imitate Socrates will be criticized both by traditionalists or "establishmentarians" (at one point in American political history they were called "antidisestablishmentarians," the longest word in the language) and by people like the Sophists, who were radical critics of the tradition and the establishment in Socrates's society. Jesus was criticized by both Pharisees and Sadducees in theology, and by both Herodian collaborationists and revolutionary Zealots in politics.

So I've told you where I'm coming from. My stance is probably unacceptably dogmatic for some readers and insufficiently dogmatic for others. If that is true, far from disturbing me, it comforts me. For that puts me in the high and palmy company of Jesus and Socrates. One cannot, of course, argue that to have opponents on opposite sides, as they did, is a guarantee of being right. But one can argue that if one is right, one will have opponents on both sides.

1

WHAT IS RELIGION?

The Problem of Definition

Bea and Thomas have just come from the first class in Professor Fesser's course on world religions.

Thomas: Well, that was a surprise!

Bea: To me too, frankly. I think I'm going to drop this course.

Thomas: Oh. Apparently your surprise was the opposite of mine. I didn't think I was going to stay, but now I think I am. I thought the professor would be vague, but he's not. He made us *think*.

Bea: You think he made us think just because he asked a question we couldn't answer and then shot down all our answers and left us hanging?

Thomas: Yes! That's exactly what Socrates used to do. And it's a lot harder than most people think it is. And more valuable.

Bea: But it didn't help us to understand the thing we all came there to understand.

Thomas: What thing is that?

Bea: The religions of the world. That's the course title, after all.

Thomas: And that's what the professor talked about. So what's your complaint?

Bea: He proved that we didn't even know what the word *religion* meant. So we don't even know what we mean when we call these things *religions*. If we can't even define the most basic term in the course, why bother taking a course in it? It's ridiculous. Throughout history we keep having arguments about religion, and we fight wars to the death about religion, but we don't even know *what it is*, what we're fighting about! It's ridiculous.

Thomas: I quite agree that that's ridiculous. So let's make it less ridiculous.

Bea: How?

Thomas: Don't you think we made any progress in doing that today?

Bea: In understanding the religions of the world, the thing this course is supposed to be about? No! In understanding what *religion* means? No!

Thomas: Don't you think it's progress to understand that we don't really understand what we thought we did understand?

Bea: I understand how that Socratic skepticism may be fun for *you*. You like to play those games.

Thomas: It's not fun and games. It's understanding. That's what you're paying big tuition bucks to this university for, isn't it?

Bea: *You* are, maybe. You just love to tear ideas apart, like Socrates, don't you?

Thomas: But the Socratic method isn't "me versus you." It's *logic*.

Bea: *Your* logic, maybe.

Thomas:	No, no, there's no such thing as "your logic" or anybody else's logic. There's just logic. Two and two still make four when it moves from one mind to another.
Bea:	I know that. I just took a course in logic.
Thomas:	What grade did you get in it?
Bea:	None of your business.
Thomas:	That's a pretty low grade—"none of your business."
Bea:	You have no way of knowing what grade I got.
Thomas:	Yes, I do. Nobody who gets an A ever labels it "none of your business."
Bea:	So you think I should have been *grateful* to the professor for undermining everything I thought I knew about what religion is?
Thomas:	Absolutely.
Bea:	Why?
Thomas:	For the same reason you should be grateful to anybody who cleans your kitchen before you cook a meal in it.
Bea:	Oh. You mean the Socratic method is kind of like garbage collection?
Thomas:	Exactly.
Bea:	Okay, but what meal can we cook up in a kitchen that's empty of food as well as garbage? Because that's the upshot of what the professor said: that we have no food in our mind's kitchen; that all our ideas about what religion is, all the ideas that we thought were "food for thought," are really only garbage. So we're left with an empty kitchen.
Thomas:	That empty kitchen is called "an open mind." Haven't you heard the news? For 2,400 years, ever since Socrates, that has proved to be the very best approach for everything you want to learn. You can't put

knowledge into a closed mind any more than you can put food into a closed mouth.

Bea: But what good is an open mouth or an open mind unless it finds some food for it to clamp down on and eat? What good is it to starve? The professor showed us that we had no logical answer to the most basic question of all about religion—the question of what it is, what the word means, how to define it, what its essential nature is. And if we can't take that very first step, how can we take the second? *You* should understand that, Mister Logic.

Thomas: Maybe we *can* take that first step. Are you *sure* we can't? We won't know until we try, will we? Do you want to give up after only one try?

Bea: Hmm . . . maybe you've got a point there, Thomas. Maybe I should stay, for one more class at least. Yeah, I think I'll give the course one more chance. I didn't learn anything valuable today, but I might next week.

Thomas: Do you really think you didn't learn anything valuable today? Don't you think it's valuable to learn that your kitchen is full of garbage, that your mind is full of ignorance and fallacies? Isn't that progress?

Bea: I wouldn't call it all garbage.

Thomas: Oh? So you think you do know what religion is?

Bea: Well, yes, I do.

Thomas: Even though you can't define it?

Bea: Yes, even though I can't define it. We know all sorts of things we can't define.

Thomas: Like what?

Bea: Like beauty, or love, or time. Can you define time, Thomas?

Thomas: I think so.

Bea: I'm waiting.

Thomas: Okay, let's say I answer "No, I can't define time." So what?

Bea: But you know what it is, what it means, don't you? In practice you know it, even though in theory you don't. You use a watch, and you live by a schedule, don't you?

Thomas: Yes, but that's different. Defining time is different from defining religion. There's no argument that proves we *can't* define time, it's just very tricky to do it. But we can't define religion. It's just a vague feeling or superstition.

Bea: Oh, so now you *are* defining it. Can you prove *that* definition?

Thomas: That's not a definition. It's too general. It's not specific enough for a definition. It doesn't say what kind of vague feeling or superstition it is, what makes it a *religious* feeling or superstition.

Bea: So take it back.

Thomas: Okay, I do. But that's what the professor proved: that we have to take back all our attempts to define religion. It looks like it can't be defined.

Bea: I don't think he proved *that* at all.

Thomas: Of course he did, and very easily too. Didn't you follow his logic? Shall we go over it again?

Bea: Yes, let's. Because I care about religion. And I think *you*, of all people, might be able to help me, even though you *don't* care about it as I do. Because you have a very logical mind.

Thomas: Thank you. But I *do* care about avoiding the world's number one superstition.

Bea: Why must everything be black or white for you?

Thomas: Not everything. But this certainly is. Because if there isn't any real object for religious belief, if there's nothing real that's religious, or Godlike, or superhuman, or supernatural, or whatever religion is about, then religion has got to be the world's number one superstition or myth or illusion. Freud even calls it a collective hallucination.

Bea: Why?

Thomas: Why did he call it a hallucination? Well, Freud's analysis of religion is . . .

Bea: No, I'm not asking about Freud, I'm asking about you. Why do you say it has to be either/or, black or white? Why does religion have to be either true or a hallucination? If you live by a hallucination, you're not just wrong, you're nuts. Are you saying religious people are all nuts?

Thomas: Did you ever see the old Jimmy Stewart movie *Harvey*?

Bea: Is that the one about the invisible rabbit?

Thomas: Yeah. Harvey the invisible thirteen-foot rabbit. It was Jimmy's best friend.

Bea: I've heard of it.

Thomas: But Jimmy wasn't four years old, he was forty. So if he really believed in Harvey, he's nuts. It's not only superstition and illusion, it's insanity.

Bea: Of course. If he really believed it and it's not there.

Thomas: But God is just a big Harvey! So to believe in God, or Nirvana, or Brahman, or Allah—whatever the indefinable religious thing is—that's at least as crazy as believing in Harvey. More so, even, because God is even bigger and more important to a believer than Harvey was to Jimmy Stewart.

Bea: No, that's a bad analogy.

Thomas: Why?

Bea: It isn't crazy to believe in God.

Thomas: Why not?

Bea: Because you can't *know* that there is no God.

Thomas: But you can't know for sure that there is no Harvey either! You can't know there are no little green men from flying saucers out there somewhere hiding behind an invisibility shield. But you can't know that there are either. So what makes more sense: to believe or not to believe in your big Harvey?

Bea: I have good reasons to believe in God.

Thomas: Are they better than Jimmy's reasons for believing in Harvey?

Bea: You bet they are.

Thomas: And I also bet you can guess what my next question is going to be.

Bea: I won't fall for your strategy, Thomas. We're not arguing about God's existence yet. We're trying to define religion before we argue about it. That's logical, isn't it?

Thomas: Yes.

Bea: And that's what the class was about today.

Thomas: Right.

Bea: Because the professor is a logical man.

Thomas: That he is.

Bea: That's why he takes one question at a time.

Thomas: And he's right.

Bea: So let's get back to his first question. Let's go over the professor's argument again. Maybe we can find a weak point. Maybe we *can* define religion after all.

Thomas: Good for you, Bea. You're starting to think logically now.

Bea: What are you, my professor?

Thomas: Sort of. I'll be yours if you'll be mine. Deal?

Bea: Deal.

Thomas: Let's see, then, what was his argument? He started with the basic logical rule about definitions: that a definition has to be "coextensive" with the term defined, neither broader nor narrower. Because it has to cover *only* the thing defined, not other things too (that would make it too broad), but it has to cover *all* the examples of the thing defined, not just some of them (that would make it too narrow). Is there anything wrong with that principle?

Bea: No.

Thomas: And then he asked us for a definition of *religion* that would obey that rule and not be either too broad or too narrow. It would be too broad if it covered some things that *weren't* religions as well as things that were; and it would be too narrow if it covered only some of the things we call religions but not all of them. Okay so far?

Bea: Yes.

Thomas: And you came up with the first attempt, remember?

Bea: Yes. I said *religion* meant worshiping some kind of god or gods. And he said that was too narrow because it didn't cover Buddhism, Taoism, and Confucianism, which don't usually have any gods.

Thomas: And everybody acknowledges that those are religions.

Bea: Right.

Thomas: And therefore religion can't be defined as worshiping gods. Did you follow that logic?

Bea: Yes. And then nobody else dared to give another answer, so I tried again. I said religion was the deepest concern of the human heart. And the professor knocked that down too.

Thomas: Do you remember why?

Bea: I thought he'd say something about the "heart" being indefinable, or "deepest" being only a metaphor, or "concern" being ambiguous . . .

Thomas: Which he certainly could have done!

Bea: But all he said was that my definition was too broad. He said it covered so many other things that nobody classifies as religions—like sex and surfing and family, and nonreligious philosophies like Marxism and Stoicism and Epicureanism.

Thomas: So what's your complaint now?

Bea: That he didn't answer his own question, he just showed us that we couldn't answer it.

Thomas: Do you know why he did that?

Bea: No, do you?

Thomas: Well, let's figure it out logically.

Bea: How?

Thomas: Well, either he knows the answer or he doesn't, right?

Bea: That's logical.

Thomas: And if he doesn't know, he can't tell us.

Bea: But in that case, why is he teaching this course?

Thomas: Maybe he wants to learn.

Bea: Then he should be paying *us* tuition. And if he *does* know, why do you think he wouldn't tell us?

Thomas: Maybe he wants us to figure it out for ourselves.

Bea: Oh.

Thomas: See? You did learn something after all.

Bea: Okay, but if that's all I'm going to learn—well, I'm not going to pay good tuition money for that.

Thomas: Who said that was all you're going to learn? Why do you think there are more classes coming?

Bea: Okay, maybe we'll learn a lot in those other classes. But if that's all we can learn about *this* question, about the definition of *religion*, then that's a bummer.

Thomas: Why?

Bea: Because now we have to give up on that question. We can't define *religion*. And then how do we learn about religions in the rest of the course without even knowing what *religion* means?

Thomas: Didn't you implicitly answer that question yourself a minute ago by your analogy with time?

Bea: How was that an answer?

Thomas: Even if we can't define it, we know what it is because we know how to use the word. And if we know what it is, even if we can't define it, we can still learn a lot about it. For instance, we can progress from Newton to Einstein, from the fallacy of absolute time to the truth of the relativity of time, even though we don't have a perfect definition of time itself. Did you disagree with that analogy?

Bea: No. In fact, I think it's a pretty good one.

Thomas: So we don't have to start with a clear, logical definition of religion either. We want to end with it, but we don't have to start with it. Even if we don't have one, we don't have to give up and become skeptics. So we can talk about religion even though we don't really know exactly what we're talking about.

Bea: I guess you're right. But that's a surprising thing for *you* to say. I know you, Thomas; you're an inveterate skeptic.

Thomas: Well, sure. But there are two kinds of skepticism: a lazy kind and a hard-working kind. The lazy kind wants to give up to save the wear and tear on the gray matter.

That's not me. The hard-working kind wants to do the opposite: to critique every idea and not *assume* it to be true. That's me.

Bea: Oh.

Thomas: Are you with me on this, Bea?

Bea: I guess so. But I wonder: can you question *everything*? Can you go anywhere without any assumptions at all?

Thomas: I think that's the *only* way to go anywhere, to make progress: to treat every idea as false until it's proved to be true. I think we should treat ideas in exactly the opposite way we treat people. We treat people as innocent until proven guilty. But the scientific method is to treat ideas as guilty until proven innocent.

Bea: So that's your assumption: the scientific method.

Thomas: Well, sure, but that's not an assumption that some idea or other is *true*, that's just a methodological assumption, a practical assumption. It's a path, not a destination.

Bea: And what's the justification for that path, that method?

Thomas: I just told you: it's practical. It works. It has worked remarkably well.

Bea: Where? In the sciences, right?

Thomas: Yes. All of them.

Bea: But religion isn't a science.

Thomas: No, and neither is astrology nor alchemy nor any other superstition, and neither is schizophrenia nor paranoia nor any other mental disorder. But we can still take a scientific attitude toward those things.

Bea: Now you're *assuming* that religion is a mental disorder.

Thomas: No, I'm not. I'm only assuming that it *might* be. But I think you're assuming that it's not.

Bea: No, I'm not just *assuming* that. I have good reasons for believing it.

Thomas: You said that before. But you didn't want to examine your reasons when I asked you what they were.

Bea: Later, maybe. But for now I just want to find out what religion is.

Thomas: Fair enough. One game at a time.

Bea: Religion is more than a game. It's the deepest thing in most people's lives.

Thomas: Yes, and that's why it's either the world's biggest truth or the world's biggest superstition. And even if we can't define it, we can target it, as we can target an animal that we're hunting, and maybe we can catch it. Are you game for hunting that game? Or are you afraid to explore the seas of your faith in the ship of reason?

Bea: I'm not afraid. Whether I stay in Professor Fesser's course or not, I'll stay in *our* course. I'll talk with you about religion any time.

Thomas: Thank you! Good for you, and good for me too.

Bea: And I think I'll stay in the professor's course too, even though I didn't get what I wanted today. Because I learned something else from class today than the definition of religion.

Thomas: You mean my Socratic "lesson one" about how little you really know?

Bea: Oh, that too, but I was thinking of something else, something more positive.

Thomas: You mean the professor's explanation of how this confused idea, the idea of "religion," originated in history?

Bea: That's a second point. But that's not what I was thinking of either. But what was that point again?

Thomas: That the term *religion* arose in history only when different religions confronted each other and they needed some generic term, some X, when they started to argue that their X was a better X than the other X.

Bea: Oh, that was an enlightening point too. I never knew that before. Wasn't that where the professor quoted from that guy who was the dean of the Harvard Divinity School some time in the last century? What was his name?

Thomas: Wilfred Cantwell Smith. His book was *The Meaning and End of Religion*. Did you get his main point?

Bea: I think so. It was that no religion in the world ever called itself a "religion" until it had to compete against other religions and needed some generic term for "that kind of thing" so that it could argue that it was a better "that kind of thing" than the other ones. So the term *religion* was imposed externally by historical circumstances instead of coming from inside the religion itself. And that was true for every religion, especially Christianity, which is the one he detailed the early history of.

Thomas: I give you an A for your summary but not for your grammar.

Bea: Why?

Thomas: You ended your last sentence with a preposition.

Bea: Ah, so ending a sentence with a preposition is something up with which you will not put?

Thomas: You plagiarized that from somebody. Churchill, I think.

Bea: You can't plagiarize a joke. They're public property.

Thomas: I accept your correction. So what's the positive point you liked? Socratic critique was point one, but you said that was negative. And the historical origin of the term *religion* was point two, but you said you were thinking of another point. So what's point three? And does it help us to define religion?

Bea: No, but it's a kind of substitute for a definition. The professor said that even if we couldn't *define* religion, deductively, we could still *describe* it, inductively, by observation of particular cases. He said that we can observe the same three dimensions of every religion in the world.

Thomas: Oh, yeah. What did he call them again?

Bea: Creed, code, and cult. Or words, works, and worship. Theology, morality, and liturgy. Every religion tells you what to believe, how to live, and how to worship or pray or meditate or do some specifically religious practice. Because those express the three powers of the human soul, or the psyche, that nearly every psychologist from Plato to Freud seems to distinguish: the intellect, the moral will, and the heart, or the feelings, or the creative imagination, or whatever that third power is. I thought that three-part description was really useful. So I'm wondering: how do you want to argue about those three things?

Thomas: What makes you think I want to argue about them?

Bea: You want to argue about everything.

Thomas: Thank you.

Bea: I didn't mean it as a compliment. But how do you disagree with me about these three things?

Thomas: I think I would take Freud's attitude toward all three of these functions of religion. Every religion says that it fulfills you in all three ways, but Freud showed that they *suppress* you in all three ways. They suppress the intellect, and they suppress the will, and they suppress the desires and the creative imagination. They limit you. They impose something on you. You let somebody else tell you what to believe and how to live and how to worship.

Bea: That's what Freud thought?

Thomas: Yes.

Bea: So that's your assumption about all religions?

Thomas: No, that's my conclusion about all religions.

Bea: Oh, so you've taken this class before? I didn't know you were already an expert. So why are you here?

Thomas: Touché, Bea. I accept your correction. It's not my expert conclusion, just my so-far conclusion, my probable conclusion, my amateur conclusion.

Bea: But even if we disagree about whether religion suppresses you or fulfills you, we can still agree about what religion looks like, about those three dimensions of it, can't we? They express three powers of the soul, or the psyche, or whatever you want to call it—the three human powers that no other animal has. And I was impressed by how the professor showed that by his examples from literature. Do you remember that part? He said that most long epics have three protagonists, and they always represent these three special powers. There's a strong-willed leader who's usually kind of egotistical, and there's an intellectual, and there's also a humble, intuitive, helpful, creative, practical guy. That's Harry Potter, Hermione, and Ron. *The Lord of the Rings* has Aragorn, Gandalf, and Frodo. Star Trek has Captain Kirk, Mister Spock, and "Bones" McCoy. Dostoyevsky's *Brothers Karamazov* has Dmitri, Ivan, and Alyosha. Even the Gospels have Jesus' inner circle of Peter, John, and James.

Thomas: I know. You don't have to go through all the examples.

Bea: I thought you'd like that point about the structure of religion mirroring the structure of the human psyche, because it's empirical, it's something we can all agree about because we can observe it, no matter what we believe about its value. It shows us something about how natural religion is, how it fits our human nature.

Thomas: Maybe. But I don't see how that pattern is going to help us decide whether religion is true or false. Hallucinations, too, have universal patterns.

Bea: That's true.

Thomas: There's a fourth point the professor made that I thought was useful.

Bea: What point?

Thomas: Well, the two of us disagree not only about whether religion is true or not, but also about how the different religions relate to each other. I'm what the professor called an "exclusivist." I think all the religions of the world contradict each other. You seem to be what he called an "inclusivist." You seem to believe them all. Isn't that right?

Bea: Yes, deep down, at least, or at their center. I think they only *seem* to contradict each other when you stay on their peripheries. When you go down below the surface and you get to the deeper level, you see that they're all really saying essentially the same thing in different words. They're all different roads up the same mountain.

Thomas: So you're an inclusivist because you say that the religions include each other instead of logically excluding each other.

Bea: Right.

Thomas: And the professor, I think, is what he called a "pluralist." He thinks religions are just different, and we can't call them either exclusive or inclusive of each other. He suggested that they may be like different animal species and we don't know them well enough to know whether they can mate or not.

Bea: Right.

Thomas: So what is the connection between those three philosophical positions about religion—exclusivism, inclusivism, and pluralism—and the three dimensions of religion that we distinguished, creed and code and cult?

Bea: I thought I saw a connection there. Give me a minute to think about it. Oh, yeah. Here it is. If you look at their creeds, different religions seem to be exclusive of each other; but if you look at their moral codes, they're inclusive of each other, or at least in massive agreement; and if you look at their cultic, religious practices, their forms of worship or prayer or contemplation or yoga, they're just different, but not incompatible.

Thomas: I think you're largely right there. That is a useful map of the religious landscape. But they're still exclusive in their creeds.

Bea: But it shows that each of the three philosophies of comparative religion has some basis in truth. There's truth everywhere. Truth is inclusive, because it's much more mysterious than you can see with your black and white logic alone.

Thomas: Is that your point? That we can just ignore logic?

Bea: No, my point is that the three dimensions of religion help to solve the controversial problem of comparative religions, how the religions relate to each other. You may be right about creeds, but I'm right about codes and cults.

Thomas: So you win by a score of two to one? Is that your argument?

Bea: No, I'm not saying it's that simple.

Thomas: But you are saying that codes and cults are more important than creeds.

Bea: I guess I am.

Thomas: I disagree with that. I say the only honest reason for anyone ever to believe anything is that it's true. That has to come first.

Bea: For you, maybe.

Thomas: For you too, I think.

Bea: No, Thomas, I don't think most people are like you. I think for most people, goodness and morality and love are more important than truth. And happiness is too. Most people seek happiness all the time, but they don't seek truth all the time.

Thomas: And you're like most people, right?

Bea: Right.

Thomas: I think I can prove you're wrong about what most people put first, Bea. Answer me just one question: Do you believe in Santa Claus? Literally, I mean.

Bea: Of course not.

Thomas: But remember when you were three and it was December. Remember how well you behaved, how good you were and how moral? And remember how happy you were? So why don't you believe in Santa Claus again? If you did, you could be so very good and so very happy, as you were when you were three.

Bea: That's just silly, Thomas.

Thomas:	Answer my silly question then: Why don't you believe in Santa Claus?
Bea:	Because I know Santa Claus isn't real.
Thomas:	My point exactly. You put truth first, even before goodness or happiness. It has to be *true* goodness and *true* happiness.
Bea:	All right, I'll admit the importance of truth if you'll admit the importance of goodness and love and happiness and beauty and joy and all those other things.
Thomas:	Of course I admit them. I just say they all have to be true.
Bea:	I don't disagree with that. But I think there are other ways to find the truth besides just logic. And I think religious experience is one of those ways.
Thomas:	Well, I've never had a religious experience, or a mystical experience, or whatever you're talking about.
Bea:	So how does that refute my "inclusivism"? It's a fact that the moralities of all the world's religions are essentially the same. They all have something like a Ten Commandments. They all teach unselfishness, and the Golden Rule, and justice, and love and mercy and compassion.
Thomas:	That doesn't prove inclusivism. Because inclusivism isn't based just on comparing the obvious moral teachings. I've read inclusivist writers, like—what's the guy's name?
Bea:	Frithjof Schuon, *The Transcendent Unity of Religions*.
Thomas:	Right. And most inclusivists argue as he does. Their inclusivism is based on the claim that all the religions are one in mystical experience. But that's another thing entirely from morality.

Bea: Well, even if you reject inclusivism, you don't have to go to the other extreme and be an exclusivist. I'm surprised at you, Thomas—I thought science made you more open minded instead of narrow minded.

Thomas: I think you're confusing two very different meanings of *exclusivism*, Bea: logical exclusivism versus salvation exclusivism. A logical exclusivism between different creeds doesn't necessarily mean that everybody who believes a false creed goes to hell.

Bea: So why aren't you a pluralist, then, like the professor?

Thomas: Because pluralism sounds like the wrong kind of skepticism. It sounds like a cop-out.

Bea: So you're critical of religion, *and* of inclusivism, *and* of pluralism.

Thomas: Yes.

Bea: And you're an exclusivist only because of logic.

Thomas: Yes.

Bea: Do you have to criticize every idea you hear except logic itself?

Thomas: No, I don't have to, I choose to.

Bea: So that's your assumption. Well, it's not mine. I like to receive my data and let it sink in before I criticize it.

Thomas: So do I.

Bea: No, I think you only receive it with your senses and your logic, not your heart or your intuition.

Thomas: We have different methods, that's true. Does that mean you don't want to stay with me in our little two-person class outside of class?

Bea: Not at all. I think we can both learn a lot from each other.

Thomas: So you'll stay?

Bea: Do you want me to?

Thomas: Yes, I do.

Bea:	How much?
Thomas:	Very much.
Bea:	Are you asking me to stay only with your mind?
Thomas:	If I say my heart is in it, will you stay?
Bea:	If you say your heart *is* in it, will you be lying?
Thomas:	Are you playing games with me, Bea?
Bea:	Why do you have to answer my question with another question?
Thomas:	Why *shouldn't* I answer your question with another question? Answer me that!
Bea:	You know, I think I'll stay—maybe just to find the answer to *that* question.

2

PRIMITIVE RELIGIONS

The Sense of the Religious

Bea: Well, Thomas, what did you think of Professor Fesser's lecture today?

Thomas: I found it very helpful.

Bea: Why?

Thomas: Because it explained something about you I never understood before.

Bea: Something about *me?* What?

Thomas: What's going on in your mind when you use all that religious language.

Bea: But his lecture wasn't about Christianity or any of the other great religions of the world that I admire. It was about primitive religions, about the primitive mindset.

Thomas: But that's what I found so helpful. All that pseudo-scientific theological mumbo-jumbo that you people use, which sounds so rational and respectable and modern—it's all just a cover for primitivism. You're a primitive, Bea. Your cover's exposed.

Bea: Are you saying that my religion is like a spy's cover? A deliberate lie?

Thomas: No, I mean something like a manhole cover, a lid on top of the monsters down there in the underground, the primitive unconscious. Everything from "Jesus Loves Me, This I Know, for the Bible Tells Me So" to the *Summa Theologica*—it's a disguise, a costume. The costume is borrowed from the sciences and from logic, but underneath the costume there's the whole kit and caboodle of primitive superstitions, the stuff that the professor was presenting today—and presenting sympathetically! I couldn't believe it; at first I thought he was playing a game with us, to egg us on to refute it. But I think he's really into this stuff, just as you are. And that means that both you and the professor are really nothing but Kalahari bushmen dressed up in modern suits. You can't judge a book by its cover, and you can't judge a person by her clothes, and you can't judge a religion by its sophisticated theology. Underneath, down there in the unconscious, there's the same superstition you find among primitives. And it's the unconscious that calls the shots; the conscious, rational mind just rationalizes it. Freud proved that.

Bea: He proved it, did he? Then how come even many scientists in his own field of psychology disagree with him?

Thomas: Freud explains that too: we believe what we want to believe. Those sophisticated theologians don't *want* to believe that all religion is a collective hallucination, so they invent explanations for their superstitions that make them seem reasonable and civilized.

Bea: So the 90 or 95 percent of Americans who say they believe there's something like God are living a hallucination?

Thomas: Frankly, yes. Religion is a vast collective hallucination that has become traditional, and your culture . . .

Bea: *My* culture? Which one is yours, then? Are you from Mars?

Thomas: *Our* culture, then. It has made religion respectable because it doesn't dare to insult our ancestors who invented it.

Bea: I see. So that's where we're different. You *do* dare to insult your ancestors. In fact, you're calling your ancestors apes if Darwin is your genealogist. Sorry to hear that about your ancestors, Thomas. As for me, I call mine human.

Thomas: Very funny, but the logical point is that your religion—all your modern religions—are just new versions of old superstitions.

Bea: Prove it. Give me evidence.

Thomas: Gladly. Will you let me answer your question by asking you a few questions? Will you let me be the attorney for the prosecution and you be my witness?

Bea: Sure. I've got nothing to hide.

Thomas: What did you do yesterday morning?

Bea: It was Sunday. I went to Mass.

Thomas: Where?

Bea: At the cathedral downtown.

Thomas: And what did you do there?

Bea: I worshiped God. Like most Americans did.

Thomas: But isn't God everywhere? Why did you go to church to worship him?

Bea: Because I believe that's where Jesus is really present, in a way he's not present anywhere else.

Thomas: And who is Jesus?

Bea: He's God incarnate; he's God become man.

Thomas: Not the man who became a god when the church divinized him?

Bea: No, the church didn't divinize him, God humanized himself.

Thomas: And you believe this God-become-man is there in that church that you went to, in a way he's not present in your backyard?

Bea: Yes. Not all Christians believe that, but Catholics do. And some Protestants too.

Thomas: How is he present in your church?

Bea: He comes to us in the sacraments, especially in the Eucharist.

Thomas: That's why you go into a church?

Bea: Yes. We go to him so that he can come to us.

Thomas: How does he come to you? What do you do when you receive the Eucharist? You open your mouth, right?

Bea: Yes. And our hearts too.

Thomas: But you can receive him into your heart any time and any place, right? But you can only receive him into your mouth in the Mass, right?

Bea: Yes.

Thomas: So you eat his body and drink his blood.

Bea: Yes.

Thomas: And he's the meaning of life, right?

Bea: Right.

Thomas: So you eat the meaning of life when you eat that little piece of bread.

Bea: It's not bread. It's Jesus.

Thomas: It looks like bread, but it's really Jesus, right? And Jesus looks like just a man, but he's really God, right?

Bea: Right.

Thomas: And you say your faith doesn't contradict reason?

Bea: It contradicts *appearances*. A lot of things contradict appearances. In science too.

Thomas: But all chemical tests prove that's just ordinary bread.

Bea: No, they don't. Chemical tests can't detect anything beyond sense appearances. That doesn't mean it isn't there.

Thomas: But we know what's there by its appearances, right? For instance, we know it's a duck because it looks like a duck, walks like a duck, and quacks like a duck. And I know you're not a duck only because you don't look like a duck or walk like a duck or quack like a duck.

Bea: Yes . . .

Thomas: But when the priest says the magic words, you believe that thing really changes from being bread to being Jesus, even though the appearances don't change, right? It still looks like bread, tastes like bread, smells like bread, but it's not bread any longer, it's Jesus' body. Isn't that what you believe?

Bea: Yes.

Thomas: And when you eat him, does he just smile and say thank you and sit there? Or does he *do* things to you?

Bea: He really does things to us.

Thomas: Things we can see?

Bea: No, things we can't see.

Thomas: What things?

Bea: Well, first of all, he gives us a share in his own very life. His divine life. That's why we're there. We share our life with him and he shares his life with us.

Thomas: But that's invisible, right?

Bea: Right.

Thomas: But it does things to you, right? It's a real power, right?

Bea: You betcha!

Thomas: Like the mana the professor was talking about in all those primitive religions. The invisible divine power we can tap into through the shaman.

Bea: Well, yes, it's similar to mana in the sense that it's a real power, and it's a real presence, and it's not visible to the senses. But it's very different from mana. It's not magic. It's not a machine, it's a person.

Thomas: Let's see if I've got this straight. You're saying it's not mana because it's not magic, and it's not magic because it's not a machine but a person—a priest—who changes bread into Jesus? But the shaman is a person too.

Bea: No, the priest doesn't do it, Jesus does it. The priest is only the instrument he uses. When the priest says, "This is my body," he doesn't mean, "This is Father Clancy's body." That was Jesus speaking. The priest is only his instrument. That's why the words have that power.

Thomas: I don't see how that's any different from what the professor said about shamans. They're the same thing as your priests. They claim to be the conduits of mana, that divine or supernatural power, as radiators are conductors of heat. That's primitive religion. How is that different from what you believe?

Bea: There's no Jesus in primitive religions.

Thomas: And you believe Jesus is really God, so he has more power than mana in primitive religions, not less, right?

Bea: Well, yes. But I don't expect you to just smile and say, "Yes, of course," to all that. It's a miracle and a mystery.

Thomas: I expected you to say that. "It's a mystery" is how you people usually fudge it when somebody asks logical questions about it. But I didn't expect you to be so frank about it. I'm glad you didn't water it down or explain it away. Because that's exactly the evidence that proves my point. You believe in a real invisible supernatural power that comes to you inside those church walls, inside that ceremony you call the Mass, from that piece of bread that you call the Eucharist.

Bea: It's not bread any longer, it's Christ.

Thomas: And you believe that because . . .

Bea: Because Christ said so: "This is my body."

Thomas: So if he said that black was white and a dog was an elephant, you'd believe him.

Bea: Yes.

Thomas: I rest my case. You're a primitive.

Bea: My religion is more than primitive religions, but it's not less.

Thomas: Okay, let's look at another dimension of this stuff: not supernatural power or supernatural matter, but supernatural time, sacred time. Do you remember what the professor said about what the Australian Aborigines call "dreamtime"?

Bea: I think so. Remind me.

Thomas: The Aborigines are the most primitive people on earth. And they believe that there is this other kind of time they call "dreamtime" or "the dreaming" that's supposed to be the eternal time, the time that's always present, the time that brings the past into the present and makes it present. It's supposed to be the time of the eternal archetypes, or the time the primal ancestors live in, or the time the gods live in.

Bea: Why does this interest you?

Thomas: Because I know something about modern physics, you see, and this religious idea is about time, which is central to physics, time being the fourth dimension. Now these Aborigines believe you can really time travel back to the time of the ancestors. And you believe the same thing! You go back two thousand years to when your God was on earth, when he was crucified. You say it's really his body that you eat and his blood that you drink. And not just in your subjective thought, in your memory, as you would remember a past historical event or some person that's dead and gone, but really, literally: you think you're really with him when you're in church there, in the present moment. You say that that event of his crucifixion still happens, or that he is still alive and still doing his thing, offering his body and blood to his father for your salvation. You see, Bea, you can't fudge it, I've read your theologians and your catechism. That's what you have to believe.

Bea: I don't want to fudge it. That *is* what I believe.

Thomas: So you believe in what you call his "real presence."

Bea: Yes.

Thomas: So this guy who died two thousand years ago made himself really present to you—to your body, not just your mind, to your tongue and your teeth—at about eleven o'clock yesterday morning.

Bea: Yes. He comes across time to us. Or maybe we go back across time to him. I don't claim to know how it works.

Thomas: Whichever way it works, whether you go back in time or he comes forward in time, there's time travel going on. So you claim the same thing the Aborigines claim: that time changes. Ordinary time becomes something like aboriginal "dreamtime." When your priest says your Mass, you actually believe that he brings you back two thousand years. And you don't call that primitive magic and superstition?

Bea: No.

Thomas: I think that's enough. *Quod erat demonstrandum.* Case closed. The witness is excused. Thank you, Miss Shaman, for explaining how reasonable and scientific and logical and nonsuperstitious your religion is.

Bea: So your supposed logical refutation consists of sarcasm?

Thomas: No, seriously, Bea, I'm grateful you were so clear and forthright. I expected you'd do a little shuffle and say it was symbolic or spiritual or a "sacred mystery" or something like that. But it's magic! You actually believe in magic. You said it wasn't magic because it was personal, but you also said that the person who does it is not the priest but God, so that makes it *more* powerful than magic, not less. So the concept of magic is not too strong for what you believe happens, it's too weak.

Bea: You could put it that way, yes.

Thomas: Do *you* put it that way? Is that what you believe?

Bea: Yes. It's not like a Coke machine, where you push the right button and you get what you want.

Thomas: I see. So, to speak in analogies, it's more like sex than like engineering.

Bea: Well, that's the analogy the mystics often use.

Thomas: And this guy who comes to you is both God and man at the same time.

Bea: Yes.

Thomas: Both eternal and temporal. Both invisible and visible. Both immortal and mortal. Both Creator and creature. At the same time.

Bea: Yes. I said that already. What's your point, Thomas?

Thomas: My point is that you're a primitive. Remember what the professor said about primitive religions not accepting our categories, our distinctions, our separations, especially the separation between heaven and earth, the supernatural and the natural? Your religion sounds exactly like that: like the most primitive religion there is!

Bea: Maybe that's not the insult you meant it to be.

Thomas: And here's another thing that makes you a primitive: primitive religion believes the world is populated with a multitude of invisible nonhuman persons—spirits. There are good spirits and evil spirits, angels and demons. And they are supposed to have great power and influence in the world and in human lives. You believe that too, don't you? You believe you have guardian angels, and you believe the dead saints see you and pray for you, right?

Bea: Well, yes, but . . .

Thomas: I see. There's a big *but* coming, right? Do me a favor. Will you let me explore the essential skeleton before I explore the big butt?

Bea: First sarcasm, now puns. Look here, Thomas, you're focusing on specific beliefs like invisible spirits and the real presence of Christ in the Eucharist, but the professor's lecture was not on specific beliefs, and it certainly wasn't on the doctrines of Christianity that you find so silly, like the divinity of Christ and the Eucharist. It was on the one big thing common to all religions: the religious sense, the sense of the sacred. That's what you don't understand. You just don't get it; you just don't have that sense. Some people are colorblind; you're just religion blind. And if you don't understand *that*, that whole dimension of the sacred, then all the details and all the specific beliefs are not going to matter. If you're colorblind, then the distinction between one color and another won't matter. You're just a modern skeptic, that's all you are.

Thomas: I insulted you by calling you primitive a minute ago, and you said that wasn't an insult. Now I'll say the same thing to you: you tried to insult me by calling me modern and skeptical, but I say that's not an insult but a compliment.

Bea: But the two insults aren't equal. I insulted you for lacking something, you insulted me for having it.

Thomas: But at least we both agree that that's the biggest difference between us and between the primitive mind and the modern mind. That's what the professor said too: the biggest difference isn't the difference between primitive religions and modern religions but between religion and no religion, or between religion and irreligion, which is the new, modern spirit. Nietzsche saw how radical it was that God was dead to modern man—not just the God of one religion but all gods, all religions.

Bea: That's right. That *is* radical; it's just as radical as Nietzsche said it was. But God isn't dead. It's Nietzsche that's dead.

Thomas: Most people are, you know.

Bea: But we're forgetting something when we're talking about the death of God or the death of the religious sense. It's not just about religion. It's not just about God, it's also about humanity. If God dies, then so does humankind, because we are made in God's image; and when you drop dead, your image in the mirror drops dead too. You're a new species, Thomas. You're a dead man. You're a spiritual corpse. You're a man without a soul, without the life of God in you, without the sense of the sacred.

Thomas: Again, thank you for the compliment, Bea. How can I have a sense of the sacred if there is nothing that's really sacred? And how can there be anything that's really sacred, really Godlike, if there is no God? That's only logical. How can you expect an atheist to have that sense of the sacred?

Bea: Thomas, I really think you're thinking backwards about yourself.

Thomas: What do you mean?

Bea: You say that you have no sense of the sacred because you're an atheist. But I say that you're an atheist because you have no sense of the sacred. You just don't understand the sacred.

Thomas: No, I'm an atheist because of something I *do* understand: science.

Bea: No, that can't be the reason. Science doesn't make you an atheist. I understand science too but I also understand the sacred, and I see no contradictions between the two.

Thomas: Then you don't understand logic!

Bea: Look, let's leave that question for another day, okay?— the question of the relation between religion and science. Let's just stay on the professor's main point today, the sense of the sacred, the thing that you find in all religions, primitive and modern, okay?

Thomas: Okay. What about it?

Bea: That it's a natural sense, like the ability to see colors. You're like one of the few people who are colorblind, and you say that the vast majority of people—who say they see colors—are hallucinating. But if nearly everybody who has ever lived has had this sense of the sacred, if that's why nearly everybody has some religion—because they all have that religious sense—then that's something that doesn't come from outside, from some historical accident. That's part of human nature. It's first, it's primordial, it's primitive. But that's not an insult.

Thomas: The fact that it's primitive doesn't prove it's true.

Bea: No, but it proves that the cause for the decline of religion has to be first of all the loss of this primordial foundation, not the rise of science. The cause of atheism is psychological, not logical.

Thomas: I don't agree. I think the rise of science is the main cause. Science explained religion away. The cause is logical, not psychological. The fear of ghosts and spirits disappears once you show people that what they explained by spirits in the past can be explained better by science in the present.

Bea: But it *didn't* disappear. Not for billions of people who still believe in both religion and science.

Thomas: It's in process of disappearing. Soon it will be gone.

Bea: That's quite a faith you have there, Thomas. You have a kind of religious faith in science.

Thomas: Well, in a sense it is. It's not religious faith, but it is a kind of faith. Science is what I believe in. But it's not blind faith—I have good reasons for trusting it. It works.

Bea: Look what you just said, Thomas. You admitted that it's a kind of faith. Because everybody needs some faith, some religion, some god. You're not an atheist; your god is science.

Thomas: Oh, come on, Bea, that's not fair: you're using religious categories to explain science.

Bea: And you're using scientific categories to explain religion.

Thomas: Look, here comes Professor Fesser. Maybe he can settle our dispute. Professor, hi. We were just discussing the point you made in class today.

Fesser: I know. I heard the last bit of your conversation. Good for you both. It really encourages a teacher to hear his students extending the classroom after hours.

Thomas: And which of us do you think is right?

Fesser: About which came first, the rise of science or the decline of the sense of the sacred?

Thomas: Yes.

Fesser: I think it's a moot point.

Thomas: Because it's like the logical question of which came first, the chicken or the egg?

Fesser: No, because in either case here we are, in modern America, which is the result of both causes together. Whatever the relationship between those two causes may be, the one I was talking about today in class was not the rise of science but the decline of the sense of the sacred.

Bea: I wanted to ask you about that in class, Professor. Weren't you talking about Europe rather than America? If over 90 percent of Americans still call themselves believers in some kind of religion, how can you say the sense of the sacred is declining?

Fesser: Because the sense of the sacred is deeper than a question of conscious, mental *belief*. Polls can't measure it. It's the sense of awe, the sense that there's something to be worshiped, something that's behind the things our five external senses perceive, something detectable only by a kind of inner x-ray vision. Take the stars, for instance. When we see them, in a sense we see the same thing the ancients saw; but in another, deeper sense we see something very different. Before modern times, no one ever called what we see in the night sky mere "outer space." They called it "the heavens." It was a worship word, an awe word. They felt the sky as full, not empty. It was more than this earth, not less.

And here's an even more radical example: sex. Once everyone saw it as sacred. Today almost no one does. My colleague in the theology department once assigned a book to his class called *Sex and Sacredness*. The point was simply to explain that sense of the sacred as it used to attach to sex. He had all the students rate each of the ten books he used in the course, and that one got by far the lowest rating, even though it's rather charmingly written. Absolutely no one understood its main point.

And here's a third example: death. We're still afraid of it, of course, but it's lost its terror, its awe. Most of us still say we believe in life after death, in heaven. But that seems to have lost its solidity, its reality. Our pictures of heaven aren't moving pictures anymore.

Have you ever seen a single movie about heaven that was moving? Where are our modern Dantes?

Oh, dear. I'm sorry. I've started to lecture again. You two were having a great debate and I just squashed it with a little lecture. Can we go back to your debate? I'd really like to hear from both of you.

Thomas: Gladly, Professor. You said in your lecture that the religious sense was never doubted until about 2,500 years ago, and that the first stage of its decay was the intellectualizing of religion, first in Greece, and then in Rome, and then in the use of Greek philosophy in Christian theology and apologetics, and finally in modern times when reason matured and became science. You said those were stages in a process—the process of using our reason more than we used that religious instinct. You called it the demythologization of the cosmos, or the disenchantment of the cosmos.

Fesser: Yes.

Thomas: So it *was* the rise of reason and science that destroyed religion.

Fesser: Maybe so, maybe not. We should talk about science's role in religion, or religion's role in science, in another class. Let's talk about this religious sense itself right now, okay? Bea, you say you understand it, right? You sense it, you have it. And Thomas doesn't have it, right?

Bea: Yes. It seems to be something like a sense of humor: some people just don't have one, and they just can't understand a joke. The *sense* isn't there, so they deny that the objects of the sense are there. They don't do that with humor—they don't deny its very existence—but some of them do that with religion. Thomas does, anyway.

Fesser: Do you agree that you just don't have that sense, Thomas?

Thomas: I don't *have* it, but I think I *understand* it. Bea thinks I don't.

Fesser: How do you understand it? I mean, what do you understand it to be? What is it?

Thomas: It's an emotion, a feeling. It's not rational.

Fesser: What kind of emotion?

Thomas: I think Freud was right about that: it's a subconscious desire, a deep desire that there be some great cosmic father who can take your father's place when he dies. Someone who can solve all your problems for you and overcome your fears, especially the two deepest: the fear of ignorance and the fear of pain and death and defeat. We just can't make it in this cruel world without Big Daddy.

Fesser: So you think ignorance and death are our two greatest fears?

Thomas: I think so.

Fesser: What about the fear of loneliness?

Thomas: Okay, that too. Big Daddy has to be there. Somebody has to be there.

Fesser: That's the religious sense, then? That's the origin of the sense of the sacred?

Thomas: Yes.

Fesser: Then how come you don't have it? Aren't you afraid of ignorance, pain, death, and loneliness?

Thomas: Of course. But I don't invent giant invisible friends to deal with it.

Fesser: How do you deal with it?

Thomas: With science. Science erases ignorance. And technology erases pain and impotence and defeat. And it extends our lifespan, though it hasn't conquered death yet. Maybe someday.

Fesser: And loneliness?

Thomas: I have a lot of friends.

Fesser: "Friends with benefits"?

Thomas: You bet.

Fesser: And how has that worked for you? Has it overcome your loneliness?

Thomas: I keep busy.

Fesser: I see.

Thomas: Are you being sarcastic, Professor?

Fesser: I'm sorry. I didn't mean to be intrusive.

Thomas: No, please feel free to give me your opinion. Do you really think I'm misunderstanding this thing, this religious sense?

Fesser: Well, let's start with how you define it. I think you are half right and half wrong when you classify it as a feeling. Because there are two very different kinds of feelings, and I think both you and Freud forget that distinction. The distinction is between cognitive and affective feelings, or between intuiting and desiring. Some feelings are like seeing.

Thomas: You mean mystical experience?

Fesser: Yes, that's one example, but it's not the only one. In mystical experience, your spirit seems to detect God, seems to see God's reality, God's presence, though not of course his visible form, because he has none. But we also have other intuitive senses. We intuit beauty, for instance, but it's notoriously hard to prove or argue about. And we intuit when another person really cares for us or really is paying attention to us, but that's hard to prove because they can fake it.

The other kind of feeling is a kind of *desire*—for instance, wishful thinking, or instinctive affection, what we have for cute kittens but not cockroaches, something that gives us subjective satisfaction, inner pleasure. Do you see the difference between these two kinds of feelings? I think we share the second kind, the feelings that are desires, with the higher animals, but I think the first kind, the intuitions, are distinctively human. Do you see that distinction, Thomas?

Thomas: I'm not sure. I thought all emotions were sub-rational, things we shared with the higher animals at least in some degree. I'll have to think more about that.

Bea: Professor, that's a distinction I never noticed before either. How would you classify *gratitude*? It's a feeling or emotion, right? And if it is, which kind? An intuition or a desire?

Fesser: Oh, definitely an intuition: a *seeing* that something is owed to somebody else. Almost a sense of duty, a moral sense. *Guilt* and a sense of obligation are distinctively human feelings too, intuitive feelings. They sense something, they see something true, something that animals do not sense.

Thomas: How can a feeling like guilt be either true or false?

Fesser: Don't little kids sometimes feel guilty when a parent or grandparent dies? That's false guilt. And don't some criminals have no sense of guilt at all? Is that true? Did any prisoner ever argue with the judge who pronounced him guilty: "But judge, I don't *feel* guilty"?

Thomas: I think I see your point. Animals feel shame but not guilt. It's distinctively human.

Fesser: Exactly. Compassion is another distinctively human feeling, a kind of empathy, putting yourself into the shoes of someone else who is suffering, intuitively understanding their pain. Without that feeling it's difficult or impossible to practice the Golden Rule, "Do unto others as you would have them do to you," because you can't put yourself in their shoes and imagine how they feel.

Thomas: Are *all* these intuitive feelings moral feelings?

Fesser: No. Here's one that isn't: the sense of the contingency of the world—that nothing in it has to be, or has to be as it is. I think that's an intuition, too, an intuition into the dependence of the universe on a Creator, a Giver of existence.

Thomas: I don't see that as a feeling. It sounds like an argument— an argument for the existence of God.

Fesser: No, it's a feeling. It's much more common than an argument.

Thomas: I don't understand.

Fesser: What happens when we have that feeling is that a creature who is contingent, who does not *have* to exist, who exists only because many other causes came together to cause him, intuitively senses that there has to be also something that is not contingent like that, something that has to exist, something that's eternal. It's not an argument, it's an immediate perception, a sense, an intuition.

Thomas: I guess I don't understand that example, but I think I do understand your point about the two different kinds of emotions, intuitions, and desires.

Bea: I see your distinction too, Professor. So *hope* would be an example of the other kind of emotion, right? A desire?

Fesser: Well, now, let's look. What we usually mean by *hope* probably is fueled by a desire that the future will turn out well. But what theologians call the theological virtue of hope—I think that's different. That's a kind of prophetic intuition that beneath all appearances and all apparent injustices, reality is just, is good, and *has* to be good, in the end. I think that's a kind of almost mystical intuition, a seeing. It's a judgment, an assertion.

Thomas: Please excuse me for disagreeing, Professor, but . . .

Fesser: I will not excuse you for disagreeing, I will praise you for it.

Thomas: Thank you. But what you call hope sounds to me simply like wishful thinking, trying to outguess the doctor when he says your disease is incurable.

Fesser: No, it's not about the doctor or the disease or even your mathematical chances for survival. It's about the universe, about objective reality. It says that reality is not indifferent to good and evil, that the last word is not Rhett Butler's "Frankly, my dear, I don't give a damn." It affirms a kind of cosmic justice in the long run.

Thomas: That sounds too existential for me to buy in to. Let's try logical categories instead, okay? Your "intuition" sounds like what the old logicians called "the first act of the mind"—simple apprehension. Understanding the meaning of a concept. Then what you said about hope sounds like the second act of the mind—a *judgment*, a truth claim, that justice will be done in the end. And morality is the claim that justice *ought* to be done. Then when you go from that to the conclusion that justice *will* be done, that sounds like an argument, which is the third act of the mind. Also, what you said about the sense of the contingency of the world moving us to affirm an absolute, a God—I think that's also the third act of the mind, looking along the evidence, reasoning, even though it's immediate and intuitive.

Fesser: That's very perceptive, Thomas, and clear and accurate too. Yes, I think that's exactly what I'm saying.

Thomas: But that's medieval thinking, not modern thinking.

Fesser: Yes, it is. Thank you.

Thomas: I didn't mean it as a compliment! What about the scientific demand for what Descartes called "clear and distinct ideas," ideas that are like integers in mathematics? In modern science that has taken the place of your vague intuition. And modern logic, based on "atomic propositions" that are either true or false—that has taken the place of ancient logic, which was based on the intuition of essences, which is what the logicians called "the first act of the mind." And reasoning as either formally valid, by the law of non-contradiction alone, or formally invalid—the kind of reasoning computers do—that has taken the place of all those old syllogisms in ancient logic. That's why what we mean by "reason" today is a lot more clean and clear and simple than what they meant in the Middle Ages or in ancient Greek philosophy.

Fesser: This is true. But perhaps that shrinking of the concept of reason is a mistake. I don't see why the ancient versions of these three acts of the mind *contradict* the modern ones. They're just *fatter*. But we can argue about that another time in a class in logic or epistemology or the history of philosophy. What we're trying to look at now is the sense of the sacred. We agreed that it was a feeling and I classified it as an intuitive feeling while you, Thomas, thought it was a desire, right?

Thomas: Right. I think you're confusing the true with the good or the beautiful. Only the true is rational. The good is good, but it's not rational. And the beautiful is beautiful but it's certainly not rational.

Fesser: But in the older, broader sense of "reason," it *is*.

Thomas: How?

Fesser: In three ways, in each of the "three acts of the mind." First, reason just *sees* beauty, perceives it. Second, reason judges things as having beauty or not. Third, reason creates beauty by the creative imagination, which is a kind of practical reasoning: reasoning how to do something.

Thomas: So you are saying that the feeling for beauty is not a desire but an insight? So it's part of your bigger, older, "fatter" meaning of "reason"?

Fesser: Yes. But it's a desire too. We love beauty; we want it when it's absent and we enjoy it when it's present.

Bea: So where does the sense of the sacred fit into this scheme?

Fesser: It's part of "reason" in the old, big sense of the word but not the new, modern sense. Like beauty, we see it, we judge it, and we reason about it. But if we don't see it first, then we can't judge it or reason about it. That's where the blockage lies: modern man just doesn't see it any more.

Bea: And whose fault is that?

Fesser: I don't know. Maybe it's a necessary, natural development, like becoming a teenager and losing the innocence of childhood. Or maybe it's not necessary but a mistake, because the sense of the sacred hasn't disappeared in the great saints, even when they've learned rational philosophy and modern science. Saints like Mother Teresa and John Paul II, and even writers like G. K. Chesterton and C. S. Lewis, respect all three of those things—religion and philosophy and science—and they do them very well. They have the sense of the sacred as strongly as primitive religions did, but they can also be very rational philosophers, and they're not ignorant of modern science.

Thomas: They're a dying breed. Dinosaurs.

Fesser: Maybe. That remains to be seen. I have no crystal ball. Do you?

Thomas: Yes! It's called a trajectory. When you plot a curve, if all the dots in the past form a parabola, you can extrapolate to where the dots will be in the future part of the curve.

Fesser: Then why have none of those predictions about the future come true?

Thomas: Which ones?

Fesser: The ones that predicted the disappearance of religion. If you look not just at our civilization but the whole world, religion is growing, not dying.

Thomas: Wait a few centuries. You'll see.

Fesser: That's a safe thing to say because none of us will be around then to be proved wrong.

Thomas: True. But it's certain to happen, eventually.

Fesser: That's quite a strong faith you have there, Thomas.

Bea: That's what I keep telling him. That science is his religion.

Fesser: And what do you mean by that, Bea? That he *does* have the sense of the sacred, but that it attaches to science instead of to religious objects?

Bea: No, not really. He has no idea what the word *sacred* means.

Fesser: So what do you mean by saying science is his religion?

Bea: I just mean he has absolute faith in science, beyond proof and beyond reason.

Thomas: It's not *beyond* reason. Trusting reason is *rational*, and trusting science is scientific. *Religion* is beyond reason. That's why I don't believe it.

Bea: But you can't prove by reason that there's nothing you can't prove by reason, and you can't prove by science that there's nothing beyond science, any more than you can prove by sight that there's nothing unseen.

Thomas: And you can't prove by reason that there *is* anything beyond reason either, anything supernatural or religious or whatever.

Fesser: It looks as if we have a standoff here. Let's try a different approach than argument for both of you just for a minute, to see where it goes, okay? Let's just ask the both of you what motivated you to take this course. What do you hope to get out of it?

Bea: I want to understand what different religions believe.

Thomas: So do I.

Fesser: There. See? Already you have a basic agreement in what you want, even if you don't have an agreement about what you *believe*. You both want to understand. And not only to understand the different religions of the world, but I'll bet you also want to understand each other's minds, don't you? Each of you wants to understand where in the world the other one is coming from, right?

a and Thomas: Right.

Fesser: You both want to listen first, then, before you argue.

Bea: Yeah. I do, anyway.

Thomas: So do I. Science does that: it listens to its data. It tests all its theories by the data. Unlike religion.

Bea: No, religion just has different data.

Fesser: See what just happened? You found something you agreed on, and then suddenly you both started saying no to the other one.

Thomas: Are you saying we shouldn't argue?

Fesser: Certainly not! But I'm saying you both should spend a little more time listening first. Good listeners are rare, and very valuable. In fact, I think that's the main motive for both of you being in this course: to listen, to try to understand what you don't understand.

Bea and Thomas: Yes. You're right.

Fesser: Then I'll see you in the next class.

3

HINDUISM

The Claims of Mystical Experience

Thomas: Well, that class was a lot more interesting than I thought it would be.

Bea: Why did you think it wouldn't be?

Thomas: I guess I was thinking it would be about the caste system and sacred cows and monkeys and gods and goddesses and fakirs doing magical rope tricks and walking on hot coals. Instead, we get a course in the psychology of Hindu mysticism.

Bea: So you find mysticism more interesting than magic?

Thomas: Yes.

Bea: Why?

Thomas: Oh, don't get me wrong. Not because I believe it. In fact, I think it's even more unbelievable than the magic tricks. It amounts to believing that there is indeed a God, a single, eternal, perfect being—*and it's you!* "*Tat tvam asi*"—"that art thou." Wow. Is there anything you could possibly say that's more unbelievable than that?

Bea: If you find it so unbelievable, why do you find it interesting?

Thomas: Precisely because it's so unbelievable. A little bit of insanity is boring, but that much is fascinating. A hundred pieces of junk is boring, but a mountain of junk a thousand feet high is fascinating. And at the top of that mountain you find that you are God! Wow.

Bea: What did you think of the roads up the mountain, the four yogas?

Thomas: Oh, I don't doubt you can find some good psychology there. Thousands of years of exploring the inner world while the West was exploring the outer world—that has to pay off somehow. Especially the four personality types that the four yogas are designed for—that sounds a little like the Myers-Briggs scheme. In fact it also sounds like the four temperaments or the "four humors" that the seventeenth-century pioneers of modern psychology inherited from the medievals. I was surprised the professor didn't make that connection. Do you know the four humors?

Bea: Yeah, we went over them in Shakespeare class.

Thomas: How did your professor explain them?

Bea: In terms of different reaction times. "Melancholic" people react to stimuli slowly, and thoughtfully, and they also change their reactions slowly. They chew on things. "Sanguine" people react to stimuli quickly and they also change their reactions quickly. They're social lions, great at parties. "Choleric" people react quickly— they can make quick decisions, so they tend to be leaders—and they stick to their decisions for a long time. They can be stubborn and courageous; they don't change quickly. They make good warriors and leaders.

And "phlegmatic" people react slowly and change quickly. They're careful and patient with new things but they're also open minded and experimental. They make good scientists.

Thomas: That makes perfect sense. Because *jnana* yoga is yoga for the melancholic, for the intellectuals; and *bhakti* yoga is for the sanguine, for the social lions, for "people people"; and *karma* yoga is for the choleric, for workaholics and leaders with strong egos; and *raja* yoga is for the phlegmatic, for the slow, patient, careful scientist who wants to survey the whole field and do all the data. Take away the mystical religious dimension and that's a useful classification of personality types. Primitive, of course, but pretty faithful to the facts, I'd say.

Bea: So the only thing you find wrong with this religion is its religion.

Thomas: Yeah, that's pretty much it.

Bea: What did you think of the Hindu psychology of "the four wants of man"?

Thomas: I liked that too, up to the fourth one, anyway. We all want pleasure; and then it's power; and then we mature to altruism and social service and duty and compassion and giving to others. But the fourth want—that's just ridiculous. I don't find in myself any desire for *sat*, *chit*, and *ananda*: infinite life, infinite understanding, and infinite joy. Yet Hindus claim that's in everybody, not just in mystics. Well, I'm living disproof of that. I'm somebody, and I'm not that.

Bea: As I said, the only thing you find wrong with this religion is its religion.

Thomas: Do *you* believe that stuff? I thought you were a Christian.

Bea: I am. But that doesn't mean "that stuff" can't be true too. It could be both/and instead of either/or.

Thomas: The psychology, maybe, but certainly not the theology.

Bea: Why not?

Thomas: Just about every reason you could possibly think of.

Bea: Such as?

Thomas: Well, let's list them off. One: Hindus believe in many gods as well as one. Two: Their supreme god is Brahman, and he's sort of everything in general and therefore nothing in particular. Pantheism. Their God has no *personality*. Three: Brahman has a dark side. He is equally Vishnu and Shiva, the Creator and the Destroyer. Four: God didn't create the world, he just dreamed it. Matter and time aren't really real. Five: The reason he did it is just play, *lila*. No purpose. And six: He keeps doing it over and over forever: the *kalpa* cycles, Brahman's endless dreaming and waking. History doesn't go anywhere. Seven: Instead of the Last Judgment and the possibility of hell as well as heaven, you just reincarnate until you're enlightened, and then you're in heaven. There is no eternal hell. I gotta admit that's a plus for Hinduism. An automatic eternal fire insurance policy. Eight: Karma, fatalism instead of free will. Nine: This god doesn't have a divine son who became a man and died to satisfy his father's wrath against us poor sinners. Ten: We're really all one big soul, Atman. We're not individuals, just lumps in a big tapioca pudding. Eleven: After death we reincarnate. A kind of cosmic recycling. Twelve, the biggie: *Tat tvam asi*. Deep down, you are Atman, and Atman is Brahman; therefore you are Brahman. You are God. That's the craziest one of all.

Bea: Why?

Thomas: Just imagine: If a Christian or a Jew or a Muslim went up to his clergyman and said he just had a mystical experience and discovered that he was God, the clergyman would send for the inquisitors or the witch hunters or the shrinks, depending on the century. But if a Hindu said that to his guru, the guru would say, "Congratulations. You finally found out." And what amazes me most is how you can say you believe all the Christian stuff is true and now you're saying that all that Hindu stuff can be true too, as if you've never heard of logic and the law of non-contradiction.

Bea: That's very neat and simple, Thomas, that list. But religion isn't neat and simple because reality isn't neat and simple, and religion is about reality.

Thomas: Wow! A syllogism. You actually argued in a syllogism. Congratulations. But you just gave a good argument *against* religion instead of for it.

Bea: How do you figure that, logic twister?

Thomas: You said reality isn't neat, right?

Bea: Yes.

Thomas: That's your way of saying it isn't logical, right?

Bea: Yes.

Thomas: Well, there's your mistake. Because reality *is* logical, and if religion isn't logical, as you admit it isn't, then it's not real. That's a syllogism too.

Bea: So there's nothing that's not logical, is that what you're saying?

Thomas: That's what I'm saying.

Bea: Am I real?

Thomas: I certainly think so.

Bea: Am I logical?

Thomas: No. But . . .

Bea: Then not everything that's real is logical.

Thomas: Oh, Bea, that's just a trick with words. You're using the word *logical* ambiguously. You don't think logically but logic can explain you. You don't understand logic but logic understands you.

Bea: Oh, so logic *understands* things now? Does logic watch over you? It sounds like it's your daddy—or your God. Do you say your prayers to logic every night?

Thomas: Okay, I used a word ambiguously, just as you did. But this arguing about logic is silly. We should be arguing about *religion*.

Bea: Yes, we should.

Thomas: And don't you agree that when we argue we ought to argue logically and not commit fallacies like the ambiguities both of us just committed?

Bea: Of course . . .

Thomas: So let's do it. I just gave you twelve logical contradictions between two of the religions of the world: Christianity and Hinduism. You say that both religions can be true. I say they contradict each other. I also say that they're both false. Two truths can't contradict each other but two falsehoods can. But let's forget whether they're true or false for now; just show me that they don't contradict each other.

Bea: Fine. Maybe I can open your closed mind a little bit anyway, though I doubt it.

Thomas: Have you got time? Twelve things is a lot to talk about.

Bea: Sure. Can you take a minute to write them down so we can remember them?

Thomas: Okay. (A minute passes.) Let's start with the first one, polytheism. Your religion condemns belief in many gods. It says there's only one. Hinduism has many gods. Why isn't that a contradiction?

Bea: Because all those many gods are just symbols for the one God. Hinduism is a monotheism. It's not literally polytheism. Literal polytheism is illogical, but symbolic polytheism isn't.

Thomas: So are you saying that the only difference is that Western religions don't use personal names like Kali and Shiva for their symbols of the one God, and Hindus do?

Bea: Exactly.

Thomas: No, the difference is more than that. Hindus pray to those symbols as if they were persons who could hear them and answer their prayers. You don't do that to your symbols—unless Jesus is just a symbol.

Bea: No, Jesus is not just a symbol. He's God himself.

Thomas: So that's a real contradiction.

Bea: It's a real difference in practice, in how the two religions address God and relate to God, yes. In Hindu terms, Hinduism and Christianity are two different yogas, two different roads up the mountain, but they're about the same God. They don't contradict each other about God himself. Both religions are monotheistic.

Thomas: But Hinduism is also polytheistic.

Bea: Yes, on the popular level.

Thomas: So it's really two religions. The mystics and the philosophers believe in one god, while the masses believe in many. That contradicts Western religions, doesn't it? In the West, everybody has to believe the same thing. Isn't that what the professor called the difference between esoteric religions, like Hinduism, and exoteric religions, like Christianity? In esoteric religions only the mystics know the ultimate truth; in exoteric religions everybody does.

Bea: Yes, that's a real difference, all right, but that's just a difference about the road, not about the destination. It's a difference in practice, in what people do to relate to God, but it's not a difference about the ultimate destination, about God himself. There are different paths up the same mountain, but at the top it's one. There's only one summit. Some writer said it well (I think it was Flannery O'Connor): "Everything that rises must converge." Different people are on different yoga paths up the mountain, and they're also on different vertical levels of the mountain. The mystics are up near the top, the masses are further down. That's why the mystics agree and the masses don't. But it's only one mountain, only one God, even if they call him by different names.

Thomas: That's not what your religion teaches. Didn't Jesus say, "I am the only way"?

Bea: He said, "I am the way, the truth, and the life." He didn't use the word *only*.

Thomas: Yes, he did. He said, "No man comes to God the Father except through me." See? I know the Bible better than you do. I don't fudge my data. And that habit comes from science, not religion.

Bea: Oh, let's not argue about science again.

Thomas: How do you explain away that contradiction? Your religion says there's only one path up the mountain, not many. Hinduism says there are many, not only one.

Bea: Jesus isn't just one of many human paths up the mountain, he's the unique divine path down.

Thomas: Well, then, *that's* the difference. But it's still a difference.

Bea: But not a *contradiction*.

Thomas: Yes, it is. "No man comes to the Father except through me." What do you do with that?

Bea: Well, you know, Thomas, to be perfectly honest, I don't know. I think there must be a hidden meaning there somewhere. Jesus can't really be as narrow minded as he seems to be in that passage.

Thomas: Why? Because he disagrees with your broad mindedness? When you and Jesus disagree, who wins? If you win, is he really your God, or are you his correcting editor?

Bea: Now you're getting sarcastic instead of logical.

Thomas: I can be both. It's a serious question.

Bea: I just don't honestly know how to answer that. . . . Oh, look, here comes the professor. Let's ask him. Professor Fesser, we were just talking about Hinduism.

Fesser: Well, good for you. Did my class raise some good questions in your mind?

Bea: Oh, yes. We were arguing about Hindu inclusivism. Thomas just can't think that way. You know, many paths up the same mountain.

Thomas: I don't see how *anybody* can think that way. The law of non-contradiction hasn't been repealed east of the Ganges, has it?

Fesser: I see we're arguing about the problem of comparative religions. We're going to spend a whole class on that problem at the end of the course.

Thomas: Why at the end instead of the beginning?

Fesser: Because we have to understand the contents of the different religions before we can know how they compare with each other.

Thomas: That makes sense. First get your data straight, then find the hypothesis that explains them best.

Bea: But in Hinduism we already have that hypothesis, don't we? The idea that all the different religions of the world are like the different yoga paths in Hinduism, paths going up different sides of the same mountain. Wasn't there a Hindu philosopher who claimed that he didn't just study the different religions of the world but actually believed and practiced and experienced every single world religion in his own life, one at a time, and claimed that he discovered that they were all true? I think his name was Radhakrishnan, or Ramakrishna, or something like that.

Fesser: Yes. That was typical. Hindus are almost always inclusivists.

Thomas: And Christians and Muslims and Orthodox Jews are exclusivists, right?

Fesser: They used to be. But today there are inclusivists and pluralists as well as exclusivists among Christian philosophers of religion. And many Jews too, though not usually the Orthodox. And even a few Muslims, especially the Sufis. Frithjof Schuon was a Sufi. So it's an open question today, a controversial question, even among Westerners. And that's why I set aside a whole class to discuss it at the end of the course.

Thomas: Fine, but I'd still like to hear your answer to my question now.

Fesser: I can't promise you answers, Thomas. I'm not the Answer Man, I'm the Question Man. I think that's the

	first job of a teacher: to get the student to really raise the question.
Thomas:	Fine. But we've already raised the question, and now I'm looking for an answer. Won't you at least help me find it?
Fesser:	I'll try. What was the question?
Thomas:	Bea said she believes both the Hindu inclusivism and the Christian exclusivism, and I asked how she could do that without contradicting herself. If Jesus is God, as she says she believes, then he can't lie. So when he said that he was the only way to God, that "no man can come to the Father except through me," that seems to exclude inclusivism. He's narrow, Hinduism is broad. Why isn't that a contradiction?
Fesser:	Well, now, let's see. Bea, you believe in Christianity, right?
Bea:	Right.
Fesser:	And the distinctive teaching of Christianity is about Christ, right?
Bea:	Right.
Fesser:	And the teaching is that he's not just another good man but the Son of God, the one Son of the one God, God incarnate, God in the flesh, God become man, right? At least that's what all the traditional creeds say. Do you believe that?
Bea:	Yes. He's divine as well as human.
Fesser:	So how do you interpret his apparently exclusivist saying?
Bea:	I don't know. I was wondering if there's some hidden meaning behind it.
Fesser:	Well, maybe there's a perfectly clear meaning behind it, and maybe we can find it in the words of the same book where he makes that apparently exclusivist claim.

Bea: That's John's Gospel, right?

Fesser: Right. In the very first chapter, he's described as "the true light, which enlightens everyone." It doesn't say that he enlightens only Christians. It says he's the one light who enlightens everybody.

Thomas: Maybe that only means that eventually everybody will be enlightened to believe in him and convert to Christianity, after the missionaries have done their work all around the world.

Fesser: No, because the Greek verb for "enlightens" is in the present progressive tense, not the future tense. It says he is already enlightening everyone. And "everyone" includes Hindus, and even atheists like you. So the claim is not that he excludes anybody but just the opposite: that he includes everybody, because he's not just one among many men but the one universal God.

Thomas: That's a neat trick, Professor.

Fesser: What do you mean?

Thomas: Taking the most narrow and exclusivist thing Jesus said and making it the most inclusive thing anyone could say. It sounds to me like you're taking the law of non-contradiction lightly just as much as Bea is.

Fesser: Not at all. It's quite logically consistent. I'm not saying whether it's true or not—that's for you to decide. But it's logically consistent. The statement you classified as exclusivist and the statement I classified as inclusivist not only don't contradict each other, but they explain each other. Whether they're true or false, they're consistent with each other.

Thomas: I still don't see that.

Fesser: Let me try to explain it again. Christianity claims that Jesus is not just a man here in time but also God, in eternity. Now, only a few people knew the man Jesus when he was here on earth, and only a few of those people believed in him. So his claim to be the only way to God sounds very narrow, if he's saying that you can't know God unless you know him as this man. And it's the same situation today as two thousand years ago: only some people have heard the Christian gospel and only some of those people believe it. So if Jesus is just a man, then his claim is indeed very narrow and exclusive. But if he's God, as Christians believe, then it can be inclusive because it means that as the eternal God Jesus enlightens every mind that he ever created, that all truth is his invention or comes from his mind. If God is inclusive and Jesus is God, then Jesus is inclusive.

Bea: That's right. And that's logical.

Thomas: I see the connection: he's inclusive because he enlightens everyone in his divine nature, from eternity. But I don't believe in any divine nature. So what does this universal "enlightenment" mean for atheists like me?

Fesser: It means—and please remember that this is what it means whether it's true or not, it's just a question of how exclusive that meaning is—it means that when you use your mind to argue for atheism and when you use the principles of logic, you are using something that came from your Creator's mind, as light comes from the sun. Christians believe that Jesus is the Logos of God, and one meaning of *logos* is "mind," or "reason." It's the Greek word behind "logic." Jesus is claiming to be as universal and timeless and absolute as logic.

Thomas: But I don't believe that.

Fesser: Of course not. But it's not self-contradictory to believe that and also to believe that he is the only Son of God and the only way to God the Father. That's all I'm saying.

Thomas: I think I see what you mean. If that man was really God—whatever that could possibly mean—then he's the one who designed all human minds in the beginning, when he supposedly banged out the Big Bang and designed evolution to produce human brains.

Fesser: Yes, that—and also that he is enlightening all minds *right now*, that all the mental light that we see with our human minds comes ultimately from the sun that is his divine mind—a kind of cosmic mind behind the cosmos, like an artist behind a work of art. I think there are many Hindu philosophers and even many secular philosophers who say the same thing. Even many scientists, like Einstein. They just don't say that it's Jesus. That's the distinctively Christian claim.

Thomas: Oh. Well, that's still a big contradiction. Christians say Jesus is God, Hindus say he's not.

Fesser: Actually, most Hindus say he is, and so are the other "avatars," the other appearances of Brahman, like Buddha and Krishna. And so, in a different degree, are all of us, even if we're not yet mystically enlightened, not yet "woke up," to use the Buddhist expression. *Tat tvam asi*, remember? We all in some mysterious way have a divine identity. That's the fundamental Hindu claim. That Jesus has a divine identity is the fundamental Christian claim. So the fundamental Hindu claim logically includes the fundamental Christian claim.

Thomas: But Christians believe he's the *only* man who's God, don't they? So the two religions still contradict each other about everybody else who ever lived except Jesus, and that's a much bigger contradiction, by more than seven billion, than a contradiction about Jesus alone.

Fesser: You argue very well, Thomas.

Bea: He argues very well, but he doesn't *see* very well. He's got a narrow squint in his face.

Thomas: And I'd really like to squint at all twelve of those contradictions between Hinduism and Christianity, if we could. That's what Bea and I are arguing about.

Fesser: Just to be sure I understand your agenda: You're not arguing about whether these twelve Hindu ideas that you jotted down on that little note card in your hand are *true*, but only about whether they contradict Christianity, is that right?

Thomas: Yes. Not that I'm hot on the trail of Christianity, or any other religion. But I think it's likely that one of us must be misunderstanding what Hinduism teaches, or what it means, if one of us thinks it contradicts Christianity and one of us thinks it doesn't.

Fesser: Do you agree with that, Bea? Whether Christianity and Hinduism contradict each other or not, you and Thomas clearly do. You contradict each other about whether the two religions contradict each other.

Bea: I guess that's right. Professor, I know you said in your first lecture that we can't really solve the problem of comparative religions until we understand each religion first in its own terms, including Hinduism. But we couldn't help raising that question of comparing them now, because those two questions—what Hinduism is and whether it contradicts Christianity—go together. If we both understood what Hinduism means, we should both be agreeing about whether it contradicts Christianity or not, right?

Thomas: And since we don't agree about that, one of us probably doesn't understand Hinduism.

Bea: Gee, I wonder which one of us you think that is.

Fesser: I'd be happy to help you both understand Hinduism, but I don't want to referee a contest between the two of you. I don't teach debate, I teach religions. In my class nobody loses and everybody wins when anybody understands anybody's mistakes, including mine.

Bea: Wow, that's great, Professor. You should put that saying on a plaque or something.

Thomas: Does that mean you think that everybody's road leads up the mountain?

Fesser: Not necessarily. It means just what it says. You should understand that easily, Thomas—that's a basic principle of scientific research. Who happens to hold the theory doesn't matter. Once a theory is proved or disproved, everybody wins.

Thomas: Oh, good. I certainly agree with that. I just wanted to be sure you weren't denying the law of non-contradiction.

Fesser: I've never met anybody who succeeded in doing that, though I've met some people who have tried to.

Thomas: So have I.

Bea: Don't look at me that way, Thomas. I never denied logic, I just said it wasn't everything.

Fesser: Can we move from your boxing match to the subject? What were these twelve points about Hinduism that you disagreed about, again? Good thing you wrote them down; we keep forgetting things if we don't.

Thomas: Here they are. We talked about the first one already, monotheism and polytheism. We also talked about

Jesus. That was point number nine. Point number two is the difference between Brahman and the God of the Bible. The God of the Bible seems to have a personality; Brahman doesn't.

Fesser: Do you agree with what Thomas just said, Bea?

Bea: Yes, but I suspect there's a deeper level under that "seems."

Fesser: Why do you think so?

Bea: I don't know, I just do.

Thomas: That's not a very good answer!

Fesser: It's honest, at least. Maybe we can find a better one together. What are the attributes of the God of the Bible? And what are the attributes of Brahman? Let's make a list.

Bea: Well, *sat*, *chit*, and *ananda* are the three attributes of Brahman in Hinduism: infinite life, or infinite being; and infinite knowledge, or infinite understanding; and infinite joy, or infinite bliss. They're all in the Bible too. In both religions the one supreme God is perfect; he has all perfections; he's everything it's better to be than not to be. So it *is* the same God.

Thomas: So that's it? That's all? Case closed?

Bea: What more do you want?

Thomas: Hinduism says God isn't a *person*. Christianity says he is. In fact, he's three persons, whatever that means.

Fesser: Actually, there are *two* opinions in Hinduism. Shankara and *jnana* yoga say what you just said, Thomas, but Ramanuja and *bhakti* yoga say the opposite.

Thomas: Well, then, we can hardly find out whether Hinduism contradicts Christianity or not, if Hinduism contradicts itself.

Bea: It's inclusive, it's "big tent."

Thomas: Well, that's nice if you're a circus and you want to include as many *people* as you can under your big tent. But it's no good if you're a philosopher or a scientist, because you just can't include as many *ideas* under the big tent of your mind as you want: the law of non-contradiction stands in your way.

Bea: I've got some shocking news for you, Thomas: people are more important than ideas.

Thomas: Therefore inclusivism is better than exclusivism?

Bea: Yes.

Thomas: No. You can't compare apples and oranges, Bea. Inclusivism of *people* is better *morally*, or psychologically, yes; but exclusivism of *ideas* is better *intellectually* if you want to find out what's true. In fact, it's *necessary*.

Fesser: That's an important distinction, Thomas, but what do you think a Hindu would say to it?

Thomas: If he has a good head on his shoulders, he would have to agree with it. Not because he's a Hindu but because he's a human being, a rational animal, a truth-seeking animal.

Fesser: Do you see anything in the Hindu concept of Brahman that would change that?

Thomas: I don't see anything anywhere that could possibly change that.

Fesser: Well, suppose you believed that Brahman wasn't distinct from the universe or distinct from you, in the depths of your Atman. Do you see the difference that would make to your concept of what truth means?

Thomas: No, I don't.

Fesser: You think of truth as objective, right? Something the mind discovers? A conformity of the mind to objective reality?

Thomas: Of course.

Fesser: Do you see why a Hindu would question that?

Thomas: I don't see how anyone *could* question that.

Fesser: But if the Hindu believes that Brahman is everything; if you and the universe are not Brahman's creation but Brahman's dream, Brahman's mind; if nothing is "outside" Brahman's mind, then how can truth be outside the mind?

Thomas: It can still be outside *our* mind.

Fesser: What if we too were Brahman?

Thomas: That just seems crazy to me. I'm no more God than I am a rhinoceros.

Fesser: What if we looked at truth not from the viewpoint of an individual ego separate from Brahman and separate from the universe, but from the viewpoint of the center, from the viewpoint of Atman? Just look at what it *means*, what it logically entails about the nature of truth, whether you *believe* it or not. What it means is that Atman is your deepest center *and* the deepest center of the universe because it's Brahman—*tat tvam asi*—and therefore both you and the universe are Brahman. Do you see the logic? If I am Atman and Atman is Brahman and therefore I am Brahman, and if Brahman *thinks* the universe rather than *creates* it—do you see the consequences for what truth means, then?

Thomas: I think I see the formal logic of it, but the content of it makes no sense to me. It means that insofar as I am Atman and therefore Brahman, I'm thinking up the universe right now instead of discovering it. I understand that if that were true, then truth would be subjective, because truth is subjective to God, so to speak. I see the connection: if all that Hinduism claims is true, then truth isn't really what I said it was—objective, outside of me, judging me, superior to me—because nothing is outside of and superior to God, and I'm God. So truth is not objective to me insofar as I am Brahman rather than the individual finite ego that I believe I am.

Fesser: Good for you, Thomas. That's a very successful attempt at a fair understanding of an idea you deeply disagree with. Do you see now how this explains how opposite ideas, even mutually contradictory ideas, can both be true to a Hindu mystic?

Thomas: I think so. They can both be true because they're both Brahman's ideas. Both parts of his dream.

Fesser: Exactly.

Thomas: That sounds to me like the best argument for atheism, the best refutation of the God idea, that I've ever heard. The Brahman-God, anyway. If God exists, then the law of non-contradiction is false. A perfect reductio ad absurdum! Because whether God exists or not is debatable, but the law of non-contradiction is not debatable.

Bea: To *you* it isn't, Thomas. Because that's your God.

Thomas: That's rhetoric, Bea, not argument.

Bea: No it isn't. You're judging the idea of God by the idea of non-contradiction, while Hindus are judging the idea of non-contradiction by the idea of God.

Thomas: Wow! What a perfect recipe for nonsense!

Fesser: Wait. Perhaps both of you see something here.

Thomas: Are you going to use Hindu logic to prove that the two of us don't really contradict each other even here, Professor?

Fesser: No, I'm just trying to get you to understand what a Hindu would say.

Thomas: So any time anyone comes up with a logical either/or, the Hindu would accept both halves of the dilemma, is that it? Both/and always trumps either/or?

Fesser: Yes, I think that is what a Hindu would say. A follower of Shankara, anyway. Especially a mystic.

Thomas: But if that's so, then everything can also be its opposite.

Fesser: Yes.

Thomas: But then both/and can also be *its* opposite, namely either/or. Non-logic can be logic.

Fesser: Yes. That necessarily follows. Hindu monism or pantheism embraces and includes everything, even its opposite, dualism. That's why Hindus say Christianity is true too. Everything is true.

Thomas: Including the fact that not everything is true.

Fesser: Yes.

Thomas: You can't break out of their spider web.

Fesser: Yes. You can't escape Brahman.

Thomas: Because everything is Brahman. Nothing is outside Brahman. Not even me or the material universe. Brahman didn't *create* humans or the universe, he *is* us and it, or we are him. He's what the Upanishads call "the one without a second."

Fesser: Yes.

Thomas: So there's no *No*. Everything is *Yes*.

Fesser: Yes.

Thomas: If I believed that, I would go insane trapped in that spider web.

Bea: That's because you see yourself as the fly, not the web.

Thomas: Yes, I do! And Brahman is the spider. The web is just him too, his stuff, his spit, his guts. The spider God that wants to eat me. That's my enemy. That's why I'm an atheist. I want to be me, not him. I have wings, and I fly away, and I keep far away from that web.

Bea: But he wants you to be *you* too!

Thomas: Sure, sure. Just as the spider wants the fly to be a fly: only so that he can eat him and turn him into a part of the spider God.

Bea: No, no. God doesn't want to eat you, he loves you.

Thomas: Sure. And spiders love flies too. "Mary loved her little lamb, and I will love her too / But not the way that Mary does; I'll love her in lamb stew."

Bea: No, it's not that kind of love.

Thomas: How do you know?

Bea: What?

Thomas: I said: How do you know?

Bea: How do I know that God is not a cannibal?

Thomas: Yes. Have you ever thought about that question? The question how you know? You just *believe*, without reason, by blind faith. I don't.

Bea: It's not *blind* faith.

Thomas: Then prove it.

Bea: I can't *prove* it. If I could prove it, it wouldn't be faith.

Thomas: See? That proves my point. It's blind faith.

Fesser: May I try to mediate this dispute?

Bea: Sure.

Thomas: Be our guest. But I'm not going to deny the law of non-contradiction.

Fesser: You don't have to. You just have to see that there's a third possible way of knowing, a way that is neither proof, which science rightly demands, nor blind faith, which you are naturally suspicious of.

Thomas: What's that?

Fesser:	Experience. Which gives us probabilities, or clues— something more than blindness and less than proof, less than perfectly clear light.
Thomas:	For instance?
Fesser:	Most of the things we all believe—and *live*—are like that. For instance, can you prove I'm not a homicidal maniac who's planning to murder you? No. Is your faith in me blind, then? No, you have good reasons for trusting me, I hope. We all believe many things we can't prove. For instance, the scientific assumption of the uniformity of nature. Can you *prove* that some cosmic change won't happen tomorrow throughout the universe to make gravity work backwards? I don't think you can *prove* that, but you have very good reason to believe it, don't you? Here's another example: Can you *prove* that other minds exist, that other people aren't very cleverly designed robots?
Thomas:	So you're talking about something between blind faith and science? Something like ordinary experience and common sense?
Fesser:	Something like that, yes.
Thomas:	Are you saying that religion fits into the same category as everyday common sense?
Fesser:	Maybe.
Thomas:	Then why doesn't everybody have the same religion?
Fesser:	That's a very good question.
Thomas:	I don't want compliments. I want answers.
Fesser:	That's why you're in this course, I hope.
Thomas:	Yes. Do you have an answer, Professor?
Fesser:	Thomas, let me try to answer that question with a question, okay?

Thomas: Okay.

Fesser: Do you think that sometimes it's best for the teacher to hold back an answer until it can be understood and appreciated by the student, as Socrates often did in his dialogues?

Thomas: I guess so. I've always admired Socrates.

Fesser: Then let me tell you that I refuse to tell you my answer to that question until after you've taken my course and explored the data that you need to understand if you're going to appreciate whatever answer to that question you come up with.

Thomas: Fair enough, Professor Socrates!

Fesser: Thank you for your faith in me, Thomas. It wasn't blind, was it?

Thomas: No. I see your point. So could you help us deal with this list of questions about Hinduism now? Briefly?

Fesser: Well, looking at this list, Thomas, I'd say we've already dealt with the most fundamental ones, the ones about God. Number one was polytheism versus monotheism, number two was pantheism, number nine was Jesus' claim to be God, and number twelve was *Tat tvam asi*, and we've been talking about all four of those already, haven't we?

Thomas: Yes, but we didn't get anywhere.

Fesser: We didn't get to the place you thought you wanted to get to, did we?

Thomas: No.

Fesser: Does that mean we didn't get anywhere?

Thomas: Uh . . . no. Not unless those two terms are identical: getting where I wanted to get to, and getting some-where. And they're not.

Fesser: I see you really are a disciple of Socrates. Good for you, Thomas.

Bea: Are you saying I'm wrong, then, Professor?

Fesser: Not at all, Bea! In fact, I was trying to explain and defend your side of the argument to Thomas: that if you believe what Hindus believe about Brahman, it makes sense to deny that the law of either/or, the law of non-contradiction, is absolute.

Bea: I still don't see that very clearly, even though Thomas did: *he* got the point right away. Yet it was *my* point you were defending, not his. Am I really stupid?

Fesser: No! But I think you think more with your right brain and he thinks more with his left. He thinks like a computer: abstract calculation. You think like an animal: intuition. Neither one is wrong, we just need to combine them.

Bea: So could you explain to me a little more about the difference between Christianity and Hinduism when they speak of truth? What's the connection between Christian theology and objective truth? And what's the connection between Hindu theology and the denial of objective truth, or the questioning of objective truth, or the transcending of objective truth? I didn't quite see the point as clearly as Thomas did.

Fesser: I think we can see that more concretely if we take up your point four: the idea of creation.

Thomas: We missed point three, Brahman's "dark side."

Fesser: Oh, I think that's pretty easy to negotiate. In the Bible God has a "dark side" too: he sends the angel of death, and he punishes and kills.

Bea: But that's not a *moral* dark side. He's not unjust.

Fesser: Neither is Brahman. That's why Brahman's world runs by *karma*, a kind of cosmic justice. In both religions God causes physical evils but not moral evils.

Thomas: Oh. I see why you say that's a pretty easy point.

Fesser: No, I don't think it's easy, I think it's quite mysterious, because for both religions it implies something like free will. Remember, the chains of karma are forged by our own free choices. In both religions justice is inescapable and in both religions we are responsible for our own moral choices.

Thomas: But doesn't karma mean fate, and doesn't fate deny free will?

Bea: No. Fate and free will don't contradict each other; they're both true.

Thomas: How can they be? Either I pull my own strings or I'm a puppet and my strings are pulled by fate.

Fesser: Doesn't every story illustrate both fate and free will? The author predestines everything in the story, yet the characters act out of their free will, otherwise there's no story, no drama.

Thomas: If the author is a transcendent Creator-God, maybe.

Fesser: And also if the author is the immanent pantheist God. Both Gods know everything, including what to us is the future.

Bea: See, Thomas, it's both/and again, not either/or.

Thomas: I'm not convinced.

Fesser: I didn't think you would be. It's not as simple and quick as I made it out to be. But we don't have time to be nuanced about all twelve points. Let's go back to the one I was on when Thomas interrupted. (By the way, it was a *good* interruption, Thomas.) We were talking about the Christian idea of creation and how that explains why Christians believe truth is objective, and why the law of non-contradiction is absolute. But in Hinduism contradictories can be true because of a different image of creation, a different image of the relationship between the One and the many, Brahman and the universe. Brahman *thinks* or *dreams* the universe and us instead of *creating* it. Do you see the connection between the two different creation images and the two different ideas of truth?

Bea: No. I don't see it at all.

Fesser: Watch closely, and I think you'll see it. Jews and Christians and Muslims believe God literally created the world out of nothing and that God and the world are *other* to each other, right?

Bea: Right.

Fesser: But Hindus don't. At least not the mystical Hindus I was talking about in class today, the ones who wrote the Upanishads. The West makes three very basic distinctions that Hinduism questions: the distinction between God and the world, the distinction between God's mind and our minds, and the distinction between our minds and the world. That's why we Westerners think truth about God and the world is objective— objective to our minds, outside our minds, other than our minds. Do you see the difference now?

Bea: I think so. Hindus see the whole world, and us too, as *inside* God, as our thoughts are inside our minds.

Fesser: Yes, that's the idea.

Bea: What a beautiful idea!

Thomas: But is it true? You can't accept an idea just because you find it beautiful. And you can't believe two beautiful ideas that contradict each other just because you want to be inclusive.

Bea: But if you don't see how beautiful it is, you won't be able to really understand it, and if you don't understand it, you won't be able to see how it's true.

Fesser: Before you two go at it again, let me say that perhaps you're both right. As Thomas says, the beauty of an idea isn't the same thing as its truth. And as Bea says, sometimes it's psychologically impossible for us to discover a truth without discovering its beauty, its coherence, its meaningfulness, its attractiveness to the mind.

Bea: Okay.

Thomas: I'm still a bit suspicious, but let's go on. No, wait. Before we go on, I want to go back to one of the points you said was easy to negotiate, Professor. That made me suspicious. But then you said it was much more nuanced, and we didn't have time to follow those nuances. That was about God having a dark side, Shiva the Destroyer as well as Vishnu the Creator. Could we go back to that for just a minute? Because I still see that as a contradiction between the Hindu God and the Christian God. You disagreed with that, and you softened the contradiction between the two Gods by distinguishing physical evil, which both Gods are responsible for, and moral evil, which neither God is responsible for. Okay, but what about something halfway in between those two kinds of good and evil? What about the dualism of life and death? Brahman is both Creator and Destroyer of life, both Vishnu and Shiva, both life and death. But the Western God is all for life, not death. His prophet says, "Choose life."

Fesser: Yes. And that is a difference. Though whether it amounts to a contradiction is another question. Maybe it is, or maybe it's just a difference in emphasis. But before we answer that question of comparing the two, we have to understand what each teaches. Do you see how this difference between the two Gods—about whether or not God has a dark side, or a death side—follows from the other difference that we just explored, the one about Hinduism questioning the Western distinctions between God, humankind, and the universe?

Thomas: Yes, I do see it, I think. The West puts even its God into its dualistic framework: he's all light and no darkness. And Hinduism puts even dualism into its God: he's darkness as well as light.

Fesser: That's very well put, Thomas.

Thomas: Well, that certainly seems to be a contradiction! How could those two Gods be the same?

Fesser: But what if the Hindu God is so one that he's one even with this opposite God, this Western God? What if all dualisms disappear? Then even the dualism between Western dualism and Eastern monism disappears!

Bea: Wow! The ultimate inclusivism!

Thomas: That makes no sense. That's just words. You're just trying to deny the law of non-contradiction. The Hindu spider is just eating the Western fly. That's not inclusivism, that's cannibalism.

Fesser: I see that *you* two, at least, remain in absolute dualism, whether *God* is or not. In fact, you two are putting yourselves into an either/or dualism about whether God is to be put into an either/or dualism or not. How ironic!

Thomas: See, Bea? I win. It's either/or, not both/and, as I said. It's either me or you, not both.

Bea: No, Thomas, it's both. I embrace you and your dualism even though you don't embrace my pantheism. So I win. No, we both win. No, God wins.

Thomas: That's just words.

Bea: No, it's minds. Your mind excludes mine, but mine includes yours. It's like in that Edwin Markham poem: "He drew a circle that shut me out- / Heretic, rebel, a thing to flout, / But love and I had the wit to win, / We drew a circle and took him in."

Thomas: Sticks and stones will break my bones but names will never hurt me.

Fesser: Do you two want to look at the other differences, or do you want to keep going round and round with each other about this inclusivism/exclusivism issue?

Thomas: *I* want to look at the data.

Bea: So do I.

Fesser: Then let's look next at *lila*. That's also connected to the next idea, the *kalpa* cycles of time, the cyclic image of time rather than the Western linear image of time with a Last Judgment at the end. Do you see the connection between *lila* and *kalpa*?

Bea: I think so. *Lila* means "play." It's why Brahman thinks up a world. The world has no further purpose: that's how it's like play. It's like a ball, not like a road. It's not utilitarian, not pragmatic, not a means to a higher end. It's not "progress."

Thomas: So does this Hindu answer to the question of why God made the world contradict the Western answer, or not?

Bea: I say no.

Thomas: And I say yes, because the Western God is a moralist, and he has a will and a moral purpose: to make people his saints. The Eastern God has no moral will, no commandments.

Bea: But in both religions God made the world even though he had no needs. He didn't make us because he was bored. He made us for our sake, not his.

Fesser: It looks like you can argue that one either way: the two ideas, Hindu and Christian, are different and also similar. You can emphasize either their difference, as exclusivists do, or their similarity, as inclusivists do. Both seem to see dimensions of the truth.

Thomas: But if there are both agreements and disagreements, then exclusivism is right, because exclusivism doesn't deny that there are some agreements, but inclusivism denies that there are any real disagreements.

Bea: It's not that simple.

Fesser: No, it's not. But Thomas has a very strong point there, I think. It takes only one real contradiction between religions to prove exclusivism. But let's go on to the next point: who Jesus is.

Thomas: Well, that point is certainly a simple either/or. Either Jesus is the one and only Son of God, as Christians say, or else he's not, as everybody else says—whether because *nobody* is the Son of God, as I say, or because *everybody* is a Son of God, as Hinduism says. There's a clear line drawn in the sand there. If anybody says Jesus is the unique Son of God, that somebody is therefore a Christian, and if he denies it, he's not.

Bea: No, because Hindus say that we're all sons of God, and that *includes* Jesus.

Thomas: But Christianity denies that anyone else is the Son of God. It says Jesus is unique.

Bea: So you say that Christians and Hindus don't differ about Jesus, then, but about everybody else?

Thomas: Yes.

Bea: But you're wrong. They don't differ about everyone else. The Christian Bible says we all have to "share in the divine nature" and become sons and daughters of God. We all have to become little Christs. That's why Jesus came to earth: to make us members of his body. If I'm your body, I'm you. If you're my body, you're me. You see, ultimately, Christianity is as mystical as Hinduism.

Thomas: Sorry, Bea, I really don't want to be you, even though you're pretty cool. I just want to be me. To me, that mysticism just looks like the spider God again, in a different disguise.

Bea: No, you don't understand: you don't *lose* your identity in him, that's where you *find* it. You're holding back because you think God is your spider and you are his fly. But he's your Shakespeare and you're his Hamlet.

Thomas: We can't argue about analogies. Analogies aren't arguments.

Bea: But you're missing the whole point of both religions, of all religions, Thomas: to get that big ego of yours off the throne. All religions are trying to do the same thing in different ways and in different words and in different theologies. Don't you see it? The only way to find yourself is to lose yourself.

Thomas: No, I don't see that. And what I do see in that makes me run the other way, because I don't want to lose my ego, because that means losing my I, and I'd define that as death, not life. That's what's going to happen to me at death, and I don't want to rush it.

Bea: No, that's physical death, the death of the body. That's bad. This is the death of the ego. That's good.

Thomas: Why is it good?

Bea: Because it's the death of the fake self, and that allows the real self to live. It's like the death of cancer cells that allows the healthy cells to live.

Thomas: I don't understand that. I'm not two selves. I'm one self. And I have one body and one mind. And I believe that both die when I die.

Fesser: Which brings up another point of dispute: what happens to us when we die? The Hindu answer is reincarnation.

Thomas: That's a kind of a second chance, right? Taking the test of life again and again until you finally pass it.

Fesser: Something like that, yes.

Thomas: Well, that's certainly an idea that contradicts Christianity. The Bible says, "It is appointed unto man once to die and after that the judgment." See? I learned my Bible when I was a kid.

Bea: No, it's not that simple. We Catholics believe in purgatory, and purgatory does the same thing as reincarnation: it gets rid of everything bad in you so you can be happy in heaven forever. Hindus say reincarnation gets rid of bad karma and Catholics say purgatory gets rid of bad habits. Both religions say essentially the same thing. They both say that at death most of us are still unfinished; that death is not the end of life and not the end of our learning process. Whether that purgatory happens in another world, after your body dies, or whether it happens in this world in another body, by reincarnation—that may be a real difference, but that's only accidental. That's only about the geography, so to speak, of *where* it happens. The two religions are making essentially the same point about what happens to us, about our destiny.

Fesser: Oops. Sorry to interrupt this little class, guys, but unfortunately I just noticed the time. I have to go. I'm already late for a faculty meeting. How I wish it was going to be one tenth as interesting as this conversation. But I'd love to meet you next week after class and do this again. Do you both want to?

Bea and Thomas: Oh, yes.

Fesser: Good. See you next week here in our little class after class, then, okay?

Bea and Thomas: Okay.

Fesser: Goodbye.

Thomas: That was a bummer of an interruption. We only got part way through our list.

Bea: That's what we'll all probably say about our bucket list when we die.

Thomas: And if reincarnation is true, as Hindus say, it doesn't matter, because there's always a second chance.

Bea: I guess that's why Hindus are so patient.

Thomas: But if reincarnation is *not* true, then there's no second chance, and everything matters. Isn't that a real difference? If you only go around once in life, you better grab the gusto.

Bea: That *does* make a difference. But is it a *contradiction*? Wouldn't it be better to include both patience *and* gusto?

Thomas: So you want to include a little exclusivism in your inclusivism?

Bea: Sure, why not? That's why you're valuable to me, Thomas.

Thomas: And you're valuable to me for the exact opposite reason: I need your opposition, even your opposition to my opposition. What an odd couple we are!

4

BUDDHISM

The Logic of Nirvana

Bea:	What an inspiring lecture that was!
Thomas:	Is there anything you *don't* find "inspiring"? You'd gush about a cockroach.
Bea:	You didn't find any wisdom in what the professor said about Buddha?
Thomas:	What I found wise, I already knew: like the importance of thought, and thinking. "All that we are is determined by our thoughts"—the first line of the *Dhammapada*. And that it's pointless to talk about God and the soul. So I didn't find those two ideas "inspiring."
Bea:	What about the four noble truths?
Thomas:	They strike me as a prescription for spiritual euthanasia.
Bea:	And Nirvana?
Thomas:	It smells like mystical hogwash to me.
Bea:	Well, I guess one out of four ain't bad.
Thomas:	What do you mean, "one out of four"?
Bea:	Well, you mentioned four points and you agreed with the first one, at least, the one about all that we are

being determined by our thoughts. We both agree with Buddha and with each other. But we disagree about God and the soul—that's point two—and about the four noble truths—that's point three—and about Nirvana—that's point four. So which of those do you want to argue about?

Thomas: How logical you have suddenly become, Bea!

Bea: Is that your answer to my question?

Thomas: Good grief, you're starting to sound like me!

Bea: As you said last week, "Sticks and stones will break my bones but names will never hurt me." Did you think I would take that as a compliment? I think I'm getting infected with your sarcasm.

Thomas: I will take that as a compliment, Bea. Thank you. And I will also answer your question.

Bea: Good. When? Before Christmas, maybe?

Thomas: Oooh, what did you drink this morning? Okay, I'll answer you. I'd like to talk about Nirvana and about the four noble truths. That's distinctively Buddhist. If we started to argue about God and the soul, we'd be here till we died—and discovered that Buddha was right, that both God and the soul were illusions or at best meaningless theoretical distractions.

Bea: And who would do that discovering, if we had no souls?

Thomas: Bea, you are amazing this morning! A logical argument! In fact, exactly the one I'd ask Buddha if I could. How can there be thinking without a thinker?

Bea: I'd ask him the same question.

Thomas: Then we agree on something.

Bea: No, I think he'd come back with a pretty good answer, and one that I could reconcile with my common-sense experience and with my Christian beliefs, even though at first they seem to contradict Buddhism.

Thomas: So you want to talk about exclusivism versus inclusivism again?

Bea: Yes, but in relation to the two things you picked out, the two distinctively Buddhist ideas of the four noble truths and Nirvana. Because, as you said, if we talked about God and the soul, we'd be here until—well, until our souls met God.

Thomas: Then we'd be here forever. Because we'll never meet what doesn't exist.

Bea: But if there's a forever, there's a God. Who else could live there? No, seriously, Thomas, let's not argue the biggie—God—let's just argue about what the professor talked about this morning, okay? About how Buddhism fits in with other religions. I say they *all* have something like the four noble truths and something like Nirvana. And I suspect you don't agree. Right?

Thomas: Right. First, though, please tell me why you think the four noble truths are not just Buddhist truths but universal truths.

Bea: That's easy. The professor explained that. All practical thinking, all thinking about practice or about problems— and that's what Buddhism is, a practice, not a theory— has to answer those four questions: What's the bad effect, the symptom? What's the bad cause, the disease? What's the good effect, the cure? What's the good cause, the treatment? The four steps of a doctor's analysis, and Buddha is the doctor of the spirit. So Buddha offers four noble truths: first, that to live is to suffer (that's the symptom); second, that the cause of suffering is selfish desire (that's the disease); third, that the cure for suffering is to extinguish selfish desire, which is what *Nirvana* means (that's the prognosis); and four, that the cause of this cure is the practice of the "noble eightfold path" of ego reduction in all eight areas of life, especially thoughts.

Thomas: Well, of course you're right in thinking that if those are the four essential practical questions, every religion gives answers to them. But their answers contradict the Buddhist answers.

Bea: How?

Thomas: Because the three Western religions—Judaism and Christianity and Islam—all say that the problem isn't suffering but sin, and the solution isn't Nirvana but something else. I'm not sure what to call it, but it's certainly not Nirvana. It's "salvation" or "faith" or "obedience to God's will" or moral virtue, or something like that. Something we can do with our own minds and wills, not some mystical experience. That's why I'm even more skeptical of Buddhism than I am of Western religions: I can at least understand them—I think—and argue with them rationally. But Nirvana just kisses rationality goodbye. It's as if Christianity and Judaism and Islam are engaged in a three-pronged civil war, and those three religions together are engaged in a world war with atheism, but Buddhism is like an invasion from outer space. It doesn't have its feet on the same earthly ground at all.

Bea: And by "earthly ground," you mean reason?

Thomas: Yeah.

Bea: But Buddhism is totally rational! The four noble truths are nothing but the scientific method applied to the number-one problem in most people's lives: suffering.

Didn't you understand the professor's explanation of them? I see you hesitating. Let me go through it again. It's all a scientific analysis of the thing everyone wants to avoid, namely suffering, by the basic principle of all scientific reasoning, the principle of causality. Combine those two distinctions—the subjective difference between pain and pleasure, suffering and happiness, and the objective difference between cause and effect—and you get the universal logic of all practical problem solving. First, we observe the effects that we hate, the pain, the symptoms. Second, we find the cause that we hate, the disease, the cause of the symptoms. Third, we find a cure, a good prognosis, an effect that we love: the healing. Fourth, we find the prescription that leads to the cure, which is the good cause that produces that good effect. Bad effect, bad cause; good effect, good cause. Symptoms, diagnosis, prognosis, prescription. See how rational and universal that is? It's the logic of all religion. Buddha did for religion what Aristotle did for philosophy: he formulated the essential form of its logic.

Thomas: Bea, I wasn't shaking my head because I forgot that the professor said that, or because I didn't understand it. I was shaking my head because I disagree with the conclusion you draw from it, which is your inclusivism again. Just because all religions have the same four-step form to their practical logic, that doesn't mean that they don't contradict each other in their content—just as the fact that all philosophies that argue have to use the same logical principles doesn't mean that different philosophies don't contradict each other. For instance, the four noble truths for Christianity are death, sin, eternal life, and faith. The four noble truths for Socrates are evil, ignorance, goodness, and wisdom. The four noble truths for Marx are class conflict, capitalism, the classless society, and the communist revolution. The four noble truths for Freud are neurosis, the dynamics of conflict between id and superego, homeostasis in the psyche, and psychoanalysis. I could go on. They're all different. One set of contents contradicts another. Only the form is universal.

Bea: No, the Buddhist *content* is universal too. That's why it's compatible with any and all of your examples. Look at the four noble truths again. Number one: the problem is suffering. True for everybody. Number two: the cause of all suffering is selfish desire. True for everybody, even though not everybody knows it. When you're selfish, you're miserable; when you're unselfish, you're happy. That's true no matter what philosophy or theology or religion or scriptures you have. Number three: to take away the effect, take away the cause. So to extinguish pain, extinguish its cause, selfish desire. That's all *Nirvana* means: "extinction"—the extinction of the effect (suffering) by extinguishing its cause. That's not Martian, or even mystical; you can verify it in experience. Number four: the way to Nirvana is the noble eightfold path—the details about how to extinguish selfish desire in each area of life where it appears. You might divide life into eight different dimensions as Buddha does if you like, or into four, or into two, or into twenty-two. But every dimension where the disease appears has to be treated. That's all. That's so wonderfully simple and logical. Everyone should be able to see it. It's all-inclusive.

Thomas: So you make Buddhism out to be mere logic and common sense, both in form and in content.

Bea: Yes.

Thomas: But it's mysticism. It says the truth can't be put into words. It says Nirvana can be described only negatively. It's "not this, not that," *neti, neti.*

Bea: But Buddha himself said it's all in the four noble truths, and when his disciple—what was his name?

Thomas: Malunkyaputta.

Bea: Yeah. Sounds like a pasta. When Malunkyaputta asked Buddha to go beyond the four noble truths and answer the four questions all Hindu philosophers had answered, in different ways, so that they're classified into six different Hindu philosophical and theological systems— when Malunkyaputta asked him that, he refused to answer, and he said that Malunkyaputta was like a man who was dying of a poisoned arrow but wouldn't let Doctor Buddha cure him until he understood everything about who shot him and why and how and where and when. Buddha transcended all the Hindu systems and all the theological differences. That's why he refused to talk about Atman or Brahman at all.

Thomas: But he explicitly contradicted Hinduism with his "no-Atman" doctrine. So he himself was an exclusivist, not an inclusivist.

Bea: No, that was just words. Words don't matter much. He was just saying that his negative words—no-Atman— did less harm, or were less misleading, than he found the Hindu positive words to be—Atman and Brahman. But he didn't care about words.

Thomas: Exactly! And that makes him a mystic, not a logician.

Bea: No, because it's all in the four noble truths, and that's pure logic.

Thomas: But when you do all that Buddha says, if you agree with the four noble truths and practice the prescription, the noble eightfold path, what does he say you'll find? You'll have a mystical transformation of consciousness and you'll see that there isn't any you and there isn't any anything except this one thing that isn't a thing at all and can't be put into words. Nirvana isn't just the extinction of suffering, and it's not just the extinction of selfish desire, it's also the extinction of ordinary rational consciousness.

Fesser: (coming up from behind them) You're quite right, Thomas.

Thomas: So which comes first, then: the mystical consciousness or the moral unselfishness? The wisdom or the compassion? The *prajna* or the *karuna*? Those are the two basic Buddhist values, right?

Fesser: Right. And some Buddhists say that if you start with the extinction of selfish desire, the effect will be the extinction of the illusion of ordinary consciousness. That's probably what original Buddhism taught. So it concentrates on the noble eightfold path, which attacks desires, and the payoff is Nirvana. But other Buddhists, for instance Zen Buddhists, say that it can work the other way around: that all you have to do is extinguish the illusion of ordinary consciousness and get enlightenment, or Nirvana, or kensho, and then your selfish desires will disappear because you'll see that there's nothing real here to desire or fear. You're in a movie theater, and suddenly you realize that all those scary wild animals on the screen that you fear, and all those beautiful sexy bodies and delicious foods that you crave, are not real but only projections of consciousness, only images on the movie screen.

Thomas: I understand that. Bea does too, I think.

Fesser: What are you two arguing about, then?

Thomas: Not whether there's a contradiction between the two kinds of Buddhism. There isn't any, if the process can work both ways. That's just a matter of which one works best for you. But the contradiction is between Buddhism and Western religions, for instance, Bea's Christianity. I don't see how she as a Christian can embrace Buddhism too.

Fesser: Why not?

Thomas: Well, for one thing Buddha denies the existence of God and the soul.

Fesser: Buddhism denies the existence of *every* thing except the one thing that can't be named because it isn't a thing.

Bea: And that's God! He doesn't have a name in Buddhism, but he has a place. Look how Buddha describes him: eternal, perfect, uncreated . . .

Thomas: But even if you call that God, it's an it, not a he.

Bea: Why can't it be both? Why can't Christians truly know the *he* of God and Buddhists truly know the *it* of God? In Christian theology God is not *just* a person (actually three Persons) but also a divine *nature*.

Thomas: But even if you can pull off that reconciling trick about God . . .

Bea: It's not a trick.

Thomas: Sorry. Even if Buddhists and Christians don't contradict each other about God, they certainly contradict each other about the soul and about the creation. Buddhism explicitly denies the existence of the soul, remember? It's their doctrine of *anatta*, the "no-soul" doctrine. And they also deny the reality of what you Christians call the creation and I call the universe. According to Buddhism, there's only one thing, whether you call it God or not. But according to Christianity (and everything we're saying about Christianity now applies equally to Judaism and Islam), there's more than one thing—there's also the world God created.

Bea: Buddhists are only saying that the soul is not a thing, just as God is not a thing. That's why Buddha rejected the two thing-words, Atman and Brahman.

Thomas: But Christianity appeals to individuals to repent and believe and hope and love. Buddhists say there is no such thing as an individual soul. How can repentance come from anything but an individual soul? Buddha denied individuality.

Bea: That's theory. Buddha rejected all theory, Hindu *or* Christian. He taught only practice. And in practice Buddha appealed to individuals, just as Jesus did. Neither Buddha nor Jesus said that anybody else could do what only you can do: you have to choose to believe. It's one individual at a time for both religions.

Thomas: How can Buddha appeal to individuals if he denies that individual souls exist?

Bea: He doesn't deny they exist, he just denies that they're things. Nothing is a separate thing.

Thomas: But what about the universe?

Bea: What about it?

Thomas: Buddhists deny that it's a thing too. Or that it contains real individual, separate things.

Bea: But they don't deny that this universe is there. That would be insanity. Nirvana doesn't make mountains and rivers disappear. It lets mountains be mountains and rivers be rivers. Remember that saying? When you first study Buddhism, mountains are just mountains and rivers are just rivers. Then, while you're studying Buddhism, mountains are no longer mountains and rivers are no longer rivers. But when you are perfect in Buddhism, mountains are mountains again and rivers are rivers again. Buddhists live in the same world we do. They're not from outer space.

Thomas: Now I'm starting to get confused.

Fesser: I admire your honesty in saying that, Thomas. Sorry to interrupt. Go ahead, Bea. You were talking about how Buddhists believe in the importance of practical, this-worldly ethics. Please keep talking. I've made a resolution today to shut up for once and just listen to you for at least ten minutes, in silence. I think that would be a very Buddhist thing to do. But that would mean that Thomas would also have to take a turn at silence for ten minutes.

Thomas: Okay, Professor. I guess I'll have to settle for Bea as my teacher for ten minutes. She claims to understand Buddhism better than I do. Okay, Bea, please explain this to me, and I promise I'll try to listen. Buddhists don't believe there are any individual substances called souls, or a single substantial soul, an *Atman*, as Hindus teach. They have this *anatta* or "no-Atman" doctrine. That means they're exclusivists, doesn't it? They define themselves over against Hinduism, as Protestants define themselves over against Catholicism. Isn't that right?

Bea: But Hindus disagree with that. They say Buddhism is another Hindu yoga. They say the disagreement is only apparent.

Thomas: Then they disagree about whether they disagree.

Bea: That's just logic. Let's not get into that.

Thomas: You can't avoid it. You can't ever get out of it.

Bea: Now look who's talking about a spider God!

Thomas: Let's stop knocking each other and start learning what Buddhism is, okay? I really want to do that. And I want you to help me. Okay?

Bea: Okay.

Thomas: So if I see Buddhism as contradicting other religions, you say I'm misunderstanding it, right?

Bea: Right.

Thomas: Well, what great agreement am I not understanding? How is Buddhism the same as Hinduism and even Christianity?

Bea: I don't think I can show you the mystical agreement, Thomas, because your mind just isn't open to that. But I think I can show you the moral agreement, at least. That's my clearest argument for inclusivism, and even you should be able to understand that. It's really very simple. Christianity attacks selfish desire just as Buddhism does. Every religion does. Christians just have another word for it: *sin*. Even if different religions have different theologies, they have the same morality. And it's not just common-sense morality either. All the religions of the world agree that you have to get that ego off the throne. That's radical. They agree about something radical. Their disagreement about morality is just about the word. Buddhists call it *tanha* and Christians call it sin.

Thomas: No, that's not just another word for the same concept, it's another concept. Sin means breaking a covenant relationship, a marriage-like relationship, between you and God. It's like spiritual divorce. Buddhists have no God, and therefore no such relationship, and therefore no such thing as sin or spiritual divorce. No bride, no bridegroom, no marriage, and no divorce. No soul, no God, no covenant, and no sin.

Bea: They don't have those *concepts*, true. And Christianity doesn't have the concept of Nirvana or the four noble truths either. But an absence doesn't mean a contradiction. And a difference doesn't mean a contradiction. I'm not saying all religions teach exactly the same thing, or that there are no empty spaces in religions that other religions can fill. I'm just saying those things don't amount to contradictions. Just because a male animal doesn't have a womb and a female animal doesn't have a penis, that doesn't mean they can't mate, or that they have to fight instead of being friends. They're both *religions*, after all, so they must be doing the same essential thing. They both call themselves ways of salvation.

Thomas: But salvation from two very different things. Buddhism claims to save you from suffering, and Christianity claims to save you from sin. And Christianity saves you from sin *through* suffering: God's Son suffering for you on the cross. And the Christian saints *embrace* suffering as a road to virtue or an imitation of Christ. So Christians embrace what Buddhists save you from! And Buddhism denies the existence of what Christianity saves you from: personal sin and hell.

Here, let me put it in two concrete pictures instead of abstract ideas. I have these two pictures in my mind. Please tell me if I'm wrong. I picture Buddhism as a big, complex machine built for one purpose—let's say it's a steam shovel meant to move dirt. And Christianity is another big machine built for a very different purpose—let's say it's a rocket launcher meant to put a man on the moon. They're not like two animals that can mate. You can't launch a rocket with a steam shovel and you can't move dirt with a rocket launcher. The purpose of the steam shovel—Buddhism—is to save you from suffering in this world. The purpose of the rocket launcher is to save you from sin and get you to heaven, which is another world. Buddhism doesn't have a heaven, another world, a supernatural, or a God, or a soul.

Bea: But that just shows that they're *different*. That doesn't prove they *exclude* each other, especially in their ethics, their practice. And I don't think they contradict each other even in their theory. The difference is not in their essence but in their words.

Thomas: No. It *is* in their essence, even in ethics. The essence of Christian ethics is *agape*, charity. The essence of Buddhist ethics is *karuna*, compassion. They're not the same. Charity is an act of reason and will. Compassion is a feeling.

Bea: But they're compatible. Compassionate feelings don't impede deliberate charity; they're powerful aids to it.

Thomas: But Buddhist "compassion" goes out to everything equally and nonjudgmentally, even animals, which Christian "charity" doesn't. Remember the story of the two Buddhist monks fishing? They were holding their lines low to the ground, and the enlightened monk got bit by a poisonous lizard. And he held his hand out to the lizard so that it could bite him again. The unenlightened monk said, "Don't you know that lizard is poisonous?" And the enlightened monk answered, "Don't you know that lizard is me?"

And there's the parable of the man and the two tigers. Remember that one? Chased by one tiger, he came to the edge of a cliff, and he let himself down the cliff by clinging to a vine, while the tiger waited for him at the top. But at the bottom of the cliff there was a second tiger waiting for him to descend. Then he saw two mice, one white and one black, gnawing the vine in two above him, one from the east and the other from the west. Just before the vine broke, he saw one big wild strawberry growing on the face of the cliff. He plucked it and ate it. That's the whole story. And the enlightened Buddhist is supposed to reply to that story: "I trust the strawberry tasted as good to the man as the man tasted to the tiger." Man and tiger and strawberry are one, not two, not three. How crazy is that, by Western standards?

Bea: You can't argue about stories. Stories don't contradict each other.

Thomas: But the values they illustrate can. And here's another contradiction: "compassion" doesn't require repentance and forgiveness of sin, as Christian "faith and hope and charity" does.

Bea: Of course there's a difference, especially on the surface. But I think if we explore these two concepts more deeply, we'll find them converging the deeper down we go. You've only begun to explore these two things,

Thomas, you haven't finished. You're not being truly scientific: you're impatient with your data, and that's why you're still in the shallows.

Thomas: Even if that's all true—and I don't think it is—and even if the ethics of Buddhism and the ethics of Christianity don't contradict each other, still the whole place and point and purpose of ethics and the moral life is utterly different in the two religions. For Buddhists, it's just to clear the mind of illusion, like wiping the dust off a mirror. For Christianity, it goes all the way up because "God is love." For Buddhism, being a moral saint is the means to Nirvana or mystical experience; for Christianity, being a saint is the end, not a means. If I'm misunderstanding either or both religions, please show me how. Perhaps you understand Buddhism better than I do.

Bea: No, I think it's not just Buddhism but Christianity that you misunderstand, Thomas.

Thomas: How?

Bea: You confuse John the Baptist with Christ.

Thomas: What do you mean by that?

Bea: John the Baptist was a prophet. He preached justice and repentance of sin. He was a moralist.

Thomas: Right. So what?

Bea: He was not the Messiah. He was just the forerunner, the ground clearer. He prepared the way.

Thomas: So?

Bea: He represents morality. Christ represents something beyond morality, something more like Buddhist "enlightenment." The moral law is *not* the highest thing for Christianity, any more than it is for Buddhism. The road to the promised land went *past* Mount Sinai, where the chosen people received the Ten Commandments.

Thomas: You mean morality is necessary but not sufficient.

Bea: Yes, that's the logical way of putting it, I guess. It's necessary only as a preparation. It's like a diving board: the way to get into the pool. But the pool isn't just a bigger diving board, and when you get into the pool you don't take the diving board with you.

Thomas: You're losing me with your analogies. The diving board is morality and the pool is . . . what?

Bea: Being a saint. Having an enlightened, compassionate, loving heart, with total peace and joy. Being the kind of person Christ was. And like Buddha was. Both went beyond morality's rules. Both sat light on the rules because both knew the rules were for the sake of something much bigger.

Thomas: What do you think about that, Professor? Do Buddha and Jesus contradict each other or not?

Fesser: Frankly, I don't know what to think.

Thomas: Welcome to the ranks of the skeptics!

Fesser: Oh, I wouldn't classify myself as a skeptic. I think I can learn genuine truths and values from both religions. But I don't claim to know whether or not they contradict each other, deep down, in the last analysis.

Bea: That's pluralism, right? Neither exclusivism nor inclusivism?

Fesser: Yes.

Bea: It sounds awfully negative. And uninspiring. And unproductive.

Fesser: Compared with inclusivism, I see why you'd say that.

Bea: Even compared with exclusivism. Exclusivism at least takes a stand. It claims to know *something*.

Fesser: Do you think Socrates was "awfully negative" and "un-inspiring" and "unproductive"?

Bea: No, I guess not. The wisdom of humility, you mean. I see that. To know that you don't know is to know something true, something valuable. I include that skepticism and pluralism in my inclusivism.

Fesser: But I think pluralism is less negative than either of you two are, because you are going at each other all the time. How can peace and agreement come that way?

Bea: You mean you want us to agree to disagree.

Fesser: Something like that, yes.

Bea: You want me to include his exclusivism. And I do. But how is your pluralism less negative than Thomas's skepticism?

Fesser: It's more inclusive. Thomas definitely excludes inclusivism. I don't.

Thomas: I don't understand, Professor. How can anybody be an inclusivist once they know the teachings of the different religions as you explained them to us in class? These inclusivists, who say that Christianity and Buddhism can include each other without contradicting themselves—do they say this can happen without Buddhists admitting that Buddhism was wrong about anything, and without Christians admitting that Christianity was wrong about anything? When Buddhists and Christians unite, do they unite by changing their religions, by compromise?

Fesser: Some do, but some don't. Bea doesn't. Right, Bea?

Bea: Right. I say that each religion may *lack* something the other one has—in fact something very important—but that only means *difference*, not *contradiction*. So neither one has to admit that it was wrong.

Thomas:	I don't understand how that's possible without contradiction. Do you, Professor?
Fesser:	To be perfectly honest, I don't claim to know what Bea knows, no. But I don't conclude, as I think you do, Thomas, that because I don't understand how it's possible, therefore it isn't.
Bea:	See, Thomas? The professor is closer to my side than to yours. If I was the kind of person who said, "I told you so," I'd say, "I told you so."
Thomas:	If you *weren't* that kind of person, you wouldn't have said that, Bea.
Fesser:	No, no, wait, you two! I didn't mean to solve the problem and end the debate. I'm as far from being able to confidently agree with you, Bea, as I am with Thomas. In fact, that's one reason I'm teaching this course: to try to learn what I didn't learn on the other side of the desk, when I was a student. I often find that I really come to understand a thing only after I teach it, not before.
Bea:	Well, I guess that means all three of us are making some progress, then.
Thomas:	You know, I think it does mean that. Not necessarily because I'm coming over to your side, Bea, but because I realize I have to do a lot more hard thinking to justify my own side. And as you said, we've only just begun. I have, anyway. The mystical stuff is beyond my pay grade. I'm a pragmatist.
Bea:	But so is Buddha! What could be more practical than this? Everybody wants what Buddha calls "bliss," total bliss, which is the opposite of suffering, right?
Thomas:	Right, but Buddha claims you get that only when you attain Nirvana, and that's mystical, not rational.

Bea: But the justification for it is totally rational. Professor, I'm going to try to explain the practical point of Buddhism to Thomas. Will you correct me if I get it wrong?

Fesser: Gladly. And meanwhile I'll be quiet and let you be the teacher.

Bea: Thanks. Thomas, look: we all want to overcome suffering, right?

Thomas: Of course. But we can't. To quote the two most famous lines of the world's richest philosopher, "You can't always get what you want" and "I can't get no satisfaction."

Bea: That's because we're not all Buddhists! No, no, don't sneer and roll your eyes at me yet. Hear me out. We want to find a road that works, that takes us from suffering to bliss, right?

Thomas: Of course.

Bea: So let's analyze suffering first. Let's look at the very essence of the problem.

Thomas: Fine.

Bea: It's a relationship between what we want—happiness, bliss, satisfaction—and what we have—unhappiness, pain, frustration. Our satisfactions are small, our desires are big. We can't always get what we want.

Thomas: Right.

Bea: So to progress from misery to bliss would be to progress from the state where our satisfaction is less than our desire to a state where it isn't, right?

Thomas: Right. That doesn't prove that Buddhism gets you there.

Bea: Patience, Thomas. Step by step, please. You're so analytical and scientific, you should love this analysis.

Thomas: I'm waiting.

Bea: Here's the analysis: progressing from suffering to bliss means progressing from an inequality between desire and satisfaction to an equality between them, right?

Thomas: Right.

Bea: So there are only two ways: either to increase satisfactions or to decrease desires.

Thomas: Right. And I prefer to increase satisfactions, thank you.

Bea: But you yourself admitted that it doesn't work! "I can't get no satisfaction," remember? So why not try the only other way?

Thomas: Because I don't feel like committing spiritual euthanasia. I don't want to kill the patient to cure the disease. I don't want to turn myself into somebody who has no *tanha*, no selfish desires, at all. And that's what Buddha wants me to do.

Bea: But why not try it? It's the only thing left. The other way just doesn't get you there.

Thomas: Where is "there"? Nirvana?

Bea: Yes.

Thomas: Well, I don't want Nirvana, thank you. I just want a little more pleasure and a little less pain.

Bea: No you don't.

Thomas: What kind of arrogance is that? You're not even my shrink; you don't know what I want.

Bea: I think I do. You want bliss. We all do. You've settled for less, but you've suppressed your deepest desire.

Thomas: You mean the desire for Nirvana?

Bea: Yes, or heaven, or God, or *mukti*. You see? All the religions aim at that same mountaintop, they just call it by different names.

Thomas: I think we'll just have to agree to disagree about that, Bea. About my longing for Nirvana, whether it exists or not in me, for one thing; and for another thing, about whether the goal of your Buddhism is the same as the goal of your Christianity. I didn't read anything about Nirvana in the New Testament.

Bea: I guess we will have to just agree to disagree, for now anyway. I hope we understand each other a little better, at least.

Fesser: I'm glad you two have reached at least a temporary truce. I hope you both keep the dialogue going in my absence.

Bea: Oh, I think we will. But it works better in your presence. Do you have to run again?

Fesser: Yes, alas. I haven't learned to bilocate yet. I'm working on it, though. There are stories in both Buddhist and Christian literature about saints doing that.

Thomas: You're kidding, right?

Fesser: About my working on bilocating? Of course.

Thomas: Oh. I thought maybe since you were always moving so fast you were trying to be in two places at once.

Fesser: *You're* kidding, right?

Thomas: Right. But what about working on becoming a saint?

Fesser: That's something we all ought to take seriously. That's not kidding.

Thomas: Seriously, Professor, how come you're always running off to a meeting?

Fesser: I'm chair of this committee . . .

Thomas: Of course, a committee. Professor, you know a lot more about history than I do: Can you tell me a single great thing in the whole history of the world that was ever accomplished by a committee?

Fesser: Oh, no, of course not. You know, the Arabs define a camel as "a horse designed by a committee."

Thomas: Why, then . . .

Fesser: Because we slaves have to obey our masters.

Thomas: Slaves? Masters?

Fesser: Oh, it's better than in the past. The masters pay the slaves today. I'm an intellectual prostitute, Thomas. The university is my pimp. I don't sell my body (nobody would ever buy that!), but I sell my mind for your tuition money. Oh, stop looking so shocked, I'm kidding. At least half kidding. Gotta go. Goodbye for now.

Bea: (as he leaves) Do you think he was half kidding about half kidding?

Thomas: That would make him a quarter kidder. Yeah, I think that's about right.

5

ZEN

The Transformation of Consciousness

Thomas: I must admit I was very surprised and impressed today. There's no religion I ever heard of that seemed to make less sense to me than Zen Buddhism, with all those wacky *koans* and weird stories. But the professor made it look almost rational!

Bea: So you believe it's probably true?

Thomas: Oh, no, not at all. I didn't say that. I said it's *rational*.

Bea: But if it's rational, it's probably true—isn't that your philosophy?

Thomas: Not at all. "All elves are gods, and all men are elves, therefore all men are gods." That's perfectly rational, logical, consistent. But none of it's true.

Bea: Oh, so all you mean is that Zen is *logical*.

Thomas: Yes. Logically consistent. And that's what I found so amazing. Because the three things I had heard that Zen Buddhism taught always struck me as the three most ridiculous ideas I ever heard.

Bea: What are the three ridiculous ideas?

Thomas: First of all, according to Buddha, there are no things, no beings, no entities, no substances. Everything is empty of substance. Everything is *sunyata*, emptiness. To put it into a three-word formula, *everything is nothing*. I'd call that metaphysical nihilism.

Second is the *anatta* doctrine, the "no soul" doctrine. I am nothing. There's no me in here anywhere. I don't exist. Buddha teaches that Descartes's most absolutely certain certainty isn't even true, much less certain. Descartes says, "I think, therefore I am." Buddha says, "I think, I meditate, and I discover that I am not." So *I am nothing*. I'd call that psychological nihilism.

The third idea is the one Buddhism shares with Hinduism, something like *tat tvam asi*. I'd call it pantheism: the idea that I am really God (though Buddha won't use that name, not even "Brahman"). So when I say that Zen teaches that we are God, I certainly don't mean the God of Western religions, the transcendent person who created the universe; but I think it's essentially the same as the Eastern God, Brahman, who's described in the Hindu Upanishads as "the one without a second." But Buddha won't use that name, that noun, as the Upanishads do, either for us or for God, either for Atman or for Brahman.

By the way, that's one reason why I can't buy an inclusivism between Western and Eastern religions: because the Eastern God is "the one without a second," but the Western God is the one *with* a second, and the second is the universe he supposedly created, and us. So if I put this third Buddhist idea into a formula, it would be *I am everything*. That Brahman-without-a-name is my secret identity. It's even better than Clark

Kent being Superman; Clark Kent is God. And so are you. I am nothing outside that God. Nothing is anything outside that. I like to call the God of Eastern pantheism "the blob god" and the God of Western theism "the snob god." One of them is a pudding and I'm just a lump in that pudding, and the other one is the absentee landlord of the slum we call the world.

Bea: Insulting but amusing. So what did you find so enlightening about today's lecture?

Thomas: How the professor put these three ridiculous ideas together logically. Any one of the three logically follows from the other two. If everything is nothing and if I am everything, then I am nothing. If I am everything and I am also nothing, then everything is nothing. And if everything is nothing and I am also nothing, then I am everything. It's amazingly consistent. It's a kind of tautology but with three terms instead of two. Almost like the Trinity. But without any distinction of three *persons*. It's not one God in three persons but one truth, one equation, in three propositions.

Bea: Hmmm . . . Zen trinitarianism? That sounds like inclusivism.

Thomas: No, the content is just the opposite: not being but non-being, nothingness. Not three distinct divine persons. Nothing distinct. Nothing personal. Nothing that's any thing. Just nothing.

Fesser: (approaching) Sounds like you classify Zen as nihilism, Thomas.

Thomas: Yes. Don't you?

Fesser: No.

Thomas: Why?

Fesser: Because nihilism is pure negation, and pure negation can't positively motivate people or give them peace or happiness. And Zen sometimes does that.

Thomas: Then its nihilistic theory contradicts its positive practice.

Fesser: No, because it's not nihilism, and it's not theory. It's not theory because it's direct experience, and it's not nihilistic because it's not absolute nothingness. It's no-*thing*-ness. No separate substances or selves.

Thomas: Okay, but it's essentially the same as Hinduism, then: pantheism, the blob God.

Fesser: No, I think that image is wrong. It's not a single super-thing either, like a big blob. It's not a thing at all. Not a person either. Not matter, not spirit, not soul. Not your blob God *or* your snob God. *Neti, neti,* "not this, not that." That was how Buddha described it.

Thomas: Well, there goes inclusivism! Buddha is saying all the other religions are wrong, then, when they name God and describe God.

Fesser: Not necessarily. They could be useful myths and metaphors and symbols.

Thomas: That may be fine for a Buddhist to say about Hindu gods or Buddhist gods—aren't there millions of them in Tibetan Buddhism?—but no Jew or Christian or Muslim will buy that. They all take their one God literally.

Fesser: But do they claim to define him?

Thomas: No.

Fesser: Why?

Thomas: Because he's infinite.

Fesser: Right. And you can't define the infinite, you can't finitize the infinite. It's mystical. You can't define the indefinable, you can't eff the ineffable. So you have to sit loose on language, you have to use symbols, myths, and metaphors. Unless you're a fundamentalist and take those symbols literally.

Thomas: As the masses do, but the sages don't?

Fesser: Yes.

Thomas: But that's not Western religion, that's Eastern esoterism. That's the belief that each religion is really two different religions, a literal one for the masses and a mystical one for the sages. So even if there's no contradiction between the two levels, the esoteric level and the exoteric level, there's still a contradiction between Eastern religions, which say there are two levels, and Western religions, which deny that.

Bea: You don't understand, Thomas: the only difference between East and West is that the East uses polytheistic symbols while the West condemns that strategy as idolatry. And that is a contradiction about the means, but not about the end. For both religious systems the end is union with Ultimate Reality, and for both religions Ultimate Reality is one, not many. The polytheistic symbols don't go all the way up.

Thomas: Okay, then what is this Ultimate Reality for Buddhists if it's not Brahman? What is this non-god or non-thing that Buddha says is nothing and everything?

Bea: That very question is the wrong one.

Thomas: The "what" question, you mean?

Bea: Yes. Because it demands a definition.

Thomas: But that was Socrates's question. That was a great question. It started philosophy.

Bea: But we're not talking about philosophy now. We're talking about something that transcends philosophy.

Thomas: Because philosophy's "what" question demands a defi-
         nition, but you can't define the infinite?

Bea: Yes. And to have two things contradict each other, you
         have to define them first. So if you can't define them,
         you can't say they contradict each other. So inclusivism
         is consistent.

Thomas: No, it isn't, because inclusivism claims to know that
         they *don't* contradict each other, and for that you also
         need to define the two things.

Fesser: May I put in a word for pluralism here? It doesn't have
         either of those two problems. Both problems stem from
         the same false premise: that we can *know* whether
         religions contradict each other or not.

Thomas: So the only solution is pluralism? Well, that was short
         and sweet.

Fesser: You are disappointed.

Thomas: Yes.

Fesser: Because you wanted answers.

Thomas: No, because I wanted questions. I thought we were
         going to get into philosophical questions instead of
         avoiding them. I had prepared a few to ask you.

Fesser: I don't want to avoid them. Give me one.

Thomas: Okay. Do you think that what Zen is talking about
         when it says that the ultimate truth, or being, or non-
         being, or whatever it is, can't be defined—do you think
         that's the same as what Thomas Aquinas was talking
         about when he said that existence was distinct from
         essence? Is Zen maybe talking about existence itself?

Fesser: Excellent question, Thomas, and I don't know the
         answer to it. There seem to be striking similarities and
         also important differences, I think, between Zen Bud-
         dhism and Thomistic metaphysics. But I'm not qualified

to answer that. Ask a Thomist. I know that one of them, Dom Aelred Graham, wrote a book titled *Zen Catholicism*, in which he gave a qualified *yes* answer to that question. Another student asked me after class today whether the Zen thing was the same as what Heidegger meant by Being (*Sein*), and I had to give the same answer: I don't know; ask a Heideggerian. Heidegger himself read D. T. Suzuki, the Zen Buddhist who popularized Zen in America, and Heidegger supposedly said that if he understood Suzuki rightly, Suzuki was trying to say the same thing Heidegger was saying. And Heidegger wrote a little dialogue called *Discourse on Thinking* that sounds very much like Zen. But I don't know . . .

Bea: You *would* pick the ultimate abstract head trip, Thomas. I was hoping we would talk about something more concrete and more interesting: those koan puzzles . . .

Thomas: They're not "koan puzzles," Bea, just koans. "Koan puzzle" is like "pizza pie." It's redundant. "Koan" *means* "puzzle" in Japanese, just as "pizza" *means* "pie" in Italian.

Bea: Oh, thank you for the correction, Mister Know-It-All. Do you really expect to understand Zen with that attitude?

Fesser: Now you're both doing exactly the opposite of what all forms of Buddhism tell you to do. Do you see how?

Thomas: She's being sarcastic.

Bea: He's being arrogant.

Fesser: You're both getting into *tanha*, "grasping," trying to win by putting the other down. Judging.

Thomas: Aren't you doing the same thing to us in the very act of saying that we're doing it to each other?

Fesser: If so, let's all just stop it.

At that point something very unexpected happened. The conversation abruptly ended, even though it had only gone on for a short time, and even though the professor did not have to run off to a meeting, as he had had to do every other day. Yet all three of them said not a word more. They didn't even speak about not speaking or brag about not bragging. All three of them just smiled, and nodded, and went their separate ways. Yet they felt less separate than they ever had before.

And when Bea and Thomas met the next day, they discussed this surprising experience.

Bea: How did you like that miracle you saw yesterday, Thomas?

Thomas: What miracle?

Bea: You were silent.

Thomas: Yeah, that was a good thing, but it wasn't a miracle.

Bea: For you, I think maybe it was.

Thomas: No, I didn't have a mystical experience.

Bea: Why was it good, then?

Thomas: Not because it was some ultimate truth in itself, which is what you and the mystics and the Zen Buddhists would say, I think.

Bea: Why, then?

Thomas: Because it set off speech and words and reason, as darkness sets off light. I fully admit that it's a really good thing to just be quiet inside, in your mind as well as your mouth. Just as it's really good to sleep every night.

Bea: Is that all?

Thomas: For me, yeah. Sorry, Bea, nothing supernatural or mystical. Nothing Buddhist.

Bea: What about *tanha*? Didn't it take away *tanha* for a while?

Thomas: *Tanha*—that's the Buddhist term for greed, right?

Bea: Grasping. Egotism. Not only competitive egotism, against anybody else. Just egotism, possession, thinking "that's *mine*"—like the seagulls in *Nemo*. Didn't you feel you were giving that up?

Thomas: No, I didn't feel anything like that. I wasn't even tempted to give away all my possessions.

Bea: But you did give up your most prized possessions, at least for a while. I mean your thoughts. Even your thoughts of exclusivism and either/or logic.

Thomas: I didn't repudiate that.

Bea: No, you didn't. Because if you had, that repudiation would have been just another thought.

Thomas: You know, you have a point there, Bea.

Bea: And so do you. You came to a point there, instead of spreading yourself around. You were just *there*, you didn't shatter that deeper self and that silence into a thousand thoughts.

Thomas: No, I don't think it was that mystical.

Bea: You stopped thinking, didn't you? You were silent inside as well as outside.

Thomas: Yes.

Bea: And it was good.

Thomas: Yes.

Bea: And you'll do it again, won't you?

Thomas: Yes.

Bea: In fact, you're coming close to it even now: three yeses, and no arguments. Only a smile, like the Cheshire cat.

Thomas: But in the Alice book, the smile remained without the cat. I don't believe that can happen.

Bea: Zen does.

Thomas: So there remains a contradiction.

Bea: Not in the reality, only in the words.

6

CONFUCIANISM
The Structure of Social Success

Thomas: That was the most disappointing class in the course so far.

Bea: Thomas, didn't you ever learn to distinguish between "it was" and "it seemed to me"? You're always making absolute statements about your relative feelings.

Thomas: No, I just base my feelings on facts. It's you who interpret facts by your feelings.

Bea: But the facts about Confucianism are so impressive! Look how well it's worked! Socially, it worked more successfully than any other social system in the world. It held together the biggest nation in the world for the longest time, and it brought China out of the "period of warring states" into two millennia of relative peace and harmony.

Thomas: But it's about as interesting and challenging as *Mister Rogers' Neighborhood*.

Bea: What's that?

Thomas: Don't you remember that kids' TV show?

Bea: Not really, it was before my time. You're a little older than me. Tell me about it.

Thomas: Mister Rogers was this sweet, insufferably *nice* guy who sounded like Confucius. What he said to kids was straight out of Chinese fortune cookies. And so is Confucius's *Analects*. That has to be the most boring religious book ever written. Nothing but clichés. You could sum it all up in two lines from a Mister Rogers song: "It's nice to be generous / nice to be nice." Gee, thanks, O greatest religious teacher of all time. Thanks for that lightning flash of heavenly brilliance. I never knew that. I always thought it was *not* nice to be nice. You see, I didn't know the law of identity: I didn't know it was good to be good, or bad to be bad, or boring to be boring.

Bea: Did you ever consider that there just might be more in it than you see? Especially given its track record of success? How can a religion work so well for two thousand years with two billion people if it's only a batch of boring platitudes?

Thomas: That's a good question.

Bea: Well? I'm still waiting for your answer.

Thomas: I guess it's because most people are boring, and they actually *prefer* boring stuff. Look at the popularity of Oprah. And Eckhart Tolle. And Joel Osteen. And pop psychology.

Bea: Okay, Thomas, I've got one more question for you. You're looking for an idea you never had before, right? Something that would startle you and challenge you, and maybe change your mind, right?

Thomas: Right.

Bea: Well, have you ever entertained the idea that you are a snob?

Thomas: I answer that question with a quotation from Kierkegaard. He says there are only two kinds of people in the world: the bores and the bored. Most people are bores. They keep busy at ordinary things, and they're satisfied, and they talk about ordinary things. They're not bored with that. And that's why they're bores. They don't bore themselves or each other, but they bore the bored. The bored, on the other hand, are the elite, the aristocracy, the intelligentsia. They bore themselves but they entertain and puzzle the bores.

Bea: And you're one of the bored elite, and Confucius is one of the proletarian bores.

Thomas: Exactly.

Bea: So you're superior to Confucius, then. So I have to repeat my question: Have you ever, for one moment in your life, entertained the possibility that you are a snob?

Thomas: Is this a course in psychology or religion?

Bea: Whenever two people get together there's a course in psychology.

Thomas: So religion is a subdivision of psychology, then?

Bea: You're avoiding the question, Thomas.

Thomas: No, I'm questioning the question.

Bea: Why are your eyes looking all around, then, instead of at me?

Thomas: Because this is the point in our conversation where Professor Fesser usually shows up and puts us back on track. I'm wondering where he is today. I guess I'll have to do his job until he shows up.

Bea: *You* have to do his job? I see. And what about me? What's my job? I have to be your slow and stupid and submissive student, I suppose. Okay, Superman, I take it back: you're not a snob, you're a super-snob.

Thomas: All this just because I said Confucius bored me!

Bea: You're avoiding the issue.

Thomas: No, Bea, *you* are. Because the issue today is not Thomas but Confucius.

Bea: Okay then, let's talk about Confucius. The professor summed him up in six words: the five main Confucian virtues, and the central theme of harmony that's common to all of them.

Thomas: You don't have to go through them again. I understand them. I'm not disagreeing with them, I'm just saying they're kindergarten stuff.

Bea: But this "kindergarten stuff" has worked better than all other advanced stuff in making the most people happy and peaceful and stable for the longest time. The Chinese people are the world's largest laboratory, and Confucianism is their experiment, and it worked.

Thomas: For them, maybe. But not for me. Or for you either, I think. Wouldn't you feel bored and stifled if you had to live in a totally Confucian society? All those rules?

Bea: I don't know. I never tried it. I never lived in China. Maybe not. Maybe all those rules would feel like a game, or a beautiful, elaborate, old-fashioned ball, a dance instead of a military drill or a prison.

Thomas: Well, do a thought experiment. Imagine yourself living in Confucian China. Try it on for size in your mind. What do you feel?

Bea: I guess my answer is: no, I don't think I would be stifled at all. I think I would be happy. In fact, I think these Confucian values are not just Confucian but universal. I think all the societies in the world would be happier if they just practiced these values. They're for everybody, they're universal, they're inclusive.

Thomas: Is there anything that's *not* universal and inclusive to you?

Bea: Oh, yes. I'm talking to him.

Thomas: So you think we'd all be happier if we lived in Confucius's spiritual neighborhood, like Mister Rogers' neighborhood, eh?

Bea: I think so.

Thomas: But that's not saying much, because it's just saying that if you're good, you'll be happy. We knew that before: it's good to be good. We'd all be happier if we all obeyed the Ten Commandments, or the Golden Rule, or the Four Cardinal Virtues, or any other obvious moral code. But we don't.

Bea: But we'd be happy if we did. It's an accurate prescription for happiness. So what's your quarrel with it, Thomas? Do you prefer misery?

Thomas: Maybe I do, if it's more interesting. Maybe being happy but bored is even worse than being miserable but interested.

Bea: That's decadent.

Thomas: Sticks and stones will break my bones . . .

Bea: Seriously, why don't you agree with Confucianism?

Thomas: I do. Everybody does. My problem is that it's boring because it's obvious that we ought to practice those virtues, and it's equally obvious that we don't. It's Morality 101: it's easy to understand but hard to obey.

Bea: So would you rather make it harder to understand so that it's easier to obey? How would you change

Confucian values? Do you want to undercut them? Nuance them? Twist them? Do a little dance around them? They're like clothes that fit, and you're bored with them, so you'd prefer to try on clothes that don't fit—is that it? Systems like the divine right of kings or Marxism or capitalism or fascism or sadomasochism or Satanism or cannibalism or some other "interesting" alternative?

Thomas: I have no quarrel with Confucius, or Moses, or Mister Rogers. I just want something more than Morality 101. Are you saying that if I can't come up with a better social system than Confucianism, I have no right to be bored with it? Because if you are saying that, then you're saying that Lao Tzu had no right to be Lao Tzu. He was so bored with Confucianism that he just up and left it, left Confucian China. That door in the Great Wall that he went through on his water buffalo: that's my door too. I'm outa here.

Bea: So you're on the other side of the Great Wall with Lao Tzu?

Thomas: Yes.

Bea: And still looking for Lao Tzu, wandering through Outer Mongolia somewhere?

Thomas: That's a pretty good description of where I am, yes. But Lao Tzu left us something a lot more interesting than the *Analects*: the *Tao Te Ching*.

Bea: Yes, he did. But it didn't give us something we could all use successfully, as Confucius did. Confucius gave us social harmony, Lao Tzu gave us nature-mysticism.

Thomas: But there's an alternative social system in Taoism too. It just doesn't have all the little legalistic details.

Bea: In the *Tao Te Ching*? Where?

Thomas: Well, just take one line: "Rule large nations as you cook small fish."

Bea: What does that mean?

Thomas: Think: how do you cook small fish? Do you put layers of crust on them, and spices? Do you keep turning them over? No, you just put them in the pan for a few minutes and eat them. Simple and natural. Small is beautiful. That's the social system I want to live in.

Bea: Libertarianism, you mean.

Thomas: You could call it that, yes.

Bea: So you classify Confucianism as legalism.

Thomas: Yes.

Bea: But if it's *natural*, if it fits human nature, then all those laws are natural laws, not unnatural or artificial laws. They describe how human nature flourishes, how we can live in harmony and happiness.

Thomas: There's a better way to do that than by laws. Laws work from outside. Better to work it out from inside.

Bea: Why can't it be both? China did it both ways. Confucianism and Taoism were like classicism and romanticism: the two halves of the Chinese spirit. Why must you always analyze things logically as either/ors? You can't row a boat with either oars. You need both oars.

Thomas: Hey, that's a better pun than mine! Okay, Bea, so once again we come down to your both/and inclusivism versus my either/or exclusivism. But both Lao Tzu and Confucius were exclusivists. Confucius admitted that he simply did not understand Lao Tzu when he met him. He called him "a dragon." And Lao Tzu was so disenchanted with Confucianism that he rode right out through that door, out of China.

Bea: That doesn't mean that they were right about each other. Or that *we* can't join them, even though they didn't join each other.

Thomas: So in choosing your inclusivism over their exclusivism, you're saying you can see further than either one of them alone can see.

Bea: Yes.

Thomas: And you called *me* a snob?

Bea: But I'm only a dwarf standing on the shoulders of giants. Didn't you ever hear that saying? To claim to see more than our ancestors did—that isn't to claim you're superior, only that you're humble enough to learn from them—from both of them. From *all* of them.

At this point Bea and Thomas, who were sitting on a bench, heard a chuckle behind them. There was Professor Fesser a few feet away. They had been so engrossed in their conversation that they had not noticed him.

Fesser: I hope you won't think me sneaky for being silent for the last few minutes, but I was just so fascinated with your conversation that I had to see where it was going of itself, without my interference. I think I was silent also for another reason: the lesson we all learned at the end of our last conversation, on Zen, remember?

Thomas: I forgive you, Professor. But since you heard our argument, I'd like to hear your reaction to it.

Fesser: That's not my style—to play the judge between two litigants.

Thomas: Could you compromise your style just this once?

Fesser: Are you sure you want that?

Thomas: Quite sure. And I'm sure Bea does too.

Bea: For once I agree with you, Thomas.

Fesser: Okay, then, you asked for it. Thomas, I admire your mind and your spirit very much, but for the first time in this course I have to say I think you simply lost the argument to Bea. That's my personal judgment, anyway. Please don't take it personally.

Thomas: Thank you for your honesty, Professor. I don't take it personally, even though I'm kind of shocked by it. But maybe that's good, because I think I'm going to have to take a second look at all that Confucian stuff that I just blew off as boring. It did work, and that's a fact, and science can't ignore facts, and I want to be as scientific as I can.

Bea: Now it's my turn to be shocked. Thomas, I was wrong about you: you're not a snob after all.

Professor Fesser stayed for another hour, but the rest of the conversation was not nearly as interesting as the other conversations had been. The form of the conversations had tended to follow their content. The conversation about Zen was almost as abrupt and short and silent as Zen itself, and the rest of the conversation about Confucianism was almost as boring and obvious common sense as the Analects *themselves. Perhaps that's because it was, like Confucianism itself, full of harmony rather than controversy and argument.*

The only thing Bea and Thomas remembered afterward about the rest of this conversation about Confucianism was the professor's remark that perhaps the fact that we in the modern West tend to find Confucianism boring and platitudinous is a sign of a civilizational death wish, since death is definitely not boring. Neither is war, for killing and being killed are two of the most effective boredom relievers we have ever invented. If we were to uninvent them and practice a Confucian peace, would we find it unendurably boring and prefer the drama of death? Thomas thought there had to be a third alternative, but he could not formulate it. Perhaps that is why he did not dispute the professor's judgment that he had lost this argument to Bea. Thomas was a very honest and demanding thinker, especially toward himself.

7

TAOISM

The Power of Nature's Way

Bea: What did you think of that class, Thomas?

Thomas: A pleasant surprise! We've studied four religions so far and three of them don't have a God: Buddhism, Confucianism, and now Taoism.

Bea: Some forms of Buddhism do. Tibetan Buddhism names thousands of gods. And Shinran's "Pure Land" sect worships Buddha as a divine savior.

Thomas: But they're exceptions. So we're left with at least three religious options for atheists or agnostics like me.

Bea: By the way, Thomas, I never directly asked you: do you classify yourself as an atheist or an agnostic?

Thomas: I think I have to be agnostic about that question.

Bea: Oh. I thought you were going to say something like, "I'm an atheist, thank God."

Thomas: You're becoming delightfully irreligious, Bea. I'll have to remember that answer next time somebody asks me.

Bea: Oh, I didn't invent it. I think I stole it from Woody Allen.

Thomas: That's okay. There's no copyright on jokes.

Bea: But I have a question about you identifying with any of those three religions. After all, they are still *religions*. So you must have something religious in you if you don't just dismiss them all as silly superstitions.

Thomas: Deep psychology isn't silly superstition. That's what Buddhism is. And neither is practical social ethics. That's Confucianism. And neither is affinity with nature. That's Taoism. Frankly, I don't see why anyone calls them *religions*.

Bea: Because Nirvana isn't just psychology. It's mysticism. And Confucianism isn't just sociology. It's "the will of heaven." And Taoism isn't just Romantic poetry. It's . . . it's Tao. It's *reality*.

Thomas: But Tao isn't a god. It's nature. It's just "the way" nature works, the nature of nature.

Bea: No. It isn't. Not what *you* mean by nature.

Thomas: What do you think I mean by nature?

Bea: The stuff science can study. Isn't that what you mean by nature?

Thomas: Well, to be perfectly honest with you, I'm not sure. Because I'm not sure whether science can study Tao. I think none of our established sciences can: you never hear cosmologists or physicists or cyberneticists talking about it.

Bea: Actually, there is a rather famous book titled *The Tao of Physics*.

Thomas: I read it. It was a pretty good read, but I didn't think it was very scientific.

Bea: So do you admit that Tao transcends science?

Thomas: Not at all. I think we just haven't formulated that science yet.

Bea: So you still say that everything can be explained by science—some science, anyway.

Thomas: Yes.

Bea: It sounds to me like you have a lot of faith in what your god can do.

Thomas: You're calling science my god?

Bea: Yes.

Thomas: That's not fair, and it's a category confusion. I don't have any god. Science is no more my god than music is, or single malt Scotch. You're imposing your religious categories on my nonreligious philosophy. That's like me imposing atheist categories on your religious philosophy—as if I were to label your denial that the universe is the only thing that exists a form of atheism.

Bea: I didn't follow that analogy.

Thomas: Okay, let me try again. I believe that there are forces, or kinds of forces, or dimensions of the universe, that current science hasn't yet discovered, or hasn't yet understood. In every age there are plenty of things that current science doesn't yet understand. It doesn't matter whether what Lao Tzu meant by Tao is one of them or not, or whether what Capra was talking about in *The Tao of Physics* is an example of them or not. But science keeps progressing and understanding more and more, including things that people used to think were beyond science, or supernatural, or religious. I believe that science will keep doing that. Its trajectory is clear, so we can predict its future in general, though not in particular. That doesn't seem such a strange belief. It's like the belief that the universe will keep expanding. Why do you use a religious term for that belief? Why do you say that means I'm worshiping science as a god? I don't believe a different religion from yours; I don't believe any religion.

Bea: Okay, Thomas, I take back my terrible insult, since you find it so unbearable: I won't call you religious. Even though I meant it as a compliment.

Thomas: Don't you think we ought to define our terms before we use them as either insults or compliments?

Bea: Yes, Socrates, we ought to define our terms. But we've been trying to do that to the term *religion* ever since this course began, and we haven't succeeded yet. So don't you think it would be more profitable—and a lot more interesting—to talk about something else—about Tao instead of about terms?

Thomas: *Tao* is a term too.

Bea: No it isn't. It's a reality. But it can't be defined. Terms can be defined, but Tao can't. Remember the first line of the *Tao Te Ching*.

Thomas: I know: "The Tao that can be told—that Tao that can be tao-ed—is not the true Tao." So are you saying that anything that can't be defined is *religious*? That "the indefinable" and "the religious" are the same?

Bea: No.

Thomas: Because if you are, then . . .

Bea: I said no.

Thomas: Okay, so do you say "religion" *can* be defined, then? If so, shouldn't we keep trying?

Bea: I'm not saying whether it can be defined or not. I'm saying that I don't want to argue about that. Because that's just linguistics. I don't want to be like the theologian who died and was offered the choice between meeting God and going to a theology lecture about God—and he chose the lecture.

Thomas: I hate to disappoint you, Bea, but I don't think we're going to meet God somewhere on this campus. Unless God is a professor. I didn't enroll in this course to meet God, I enrolled in it to understand religion, and I'm disappointed that you don't care much about defining it, and that you think we can't ever define it.

Bea: I didn't say that. Maybe we can. I just said I didn't want to stay on that topic now. I'd rather talk about Tao.

Thomas: Fine.

Bea: But the first thing to understand about Tao is the first line of the book: that it can't be defined, whether you call it Tao or the will of heaven or Nirvana or Brahman or Allah or Jehovah.

Thomas: Okay—and are you saying that all those words are names for the same thing?

Bea: I don't know.

Thomas: Oh.

Bea: You sound surprised.

Thomas: I thought you'd say yes. I thought you did claim to know that. That's the first time I ever heard you doubt your universalism and inclusivism. Is that what you're doing now?

Bea: I . . . I don't know. . . . Sometimes you confuse me, Thomas.

Thomas: Thank you for the compliment!

Bea: But we're both doing the same thing now: the thing the professor warned us about the first day of class, remember? We're arguing about how the different religions are related without knowing what each of them is, what each of them says.

Thomas: You're right. We're ignoring our data.

Bea: And you're insisting that we should work deductively, from the top down, from a universal principle, starting from a universal definition of *religion* that you want to find first. But the professor said we have to work inductively, not deductively; from particular data, from the bottom up instead of from the top down.

Thomas: You're right again, Bea. Okay, let's do it. Let's do Tao.

Bea: Okay, but you can't "do" Tao.

Thomas: Aw, that's too bad. It sounds so cool: "Did you do Tao today?"

Bea: And that's significant; that silly error is significant.

Thomas: How?

Bea: Because it tries to make Tao an *object* of something that we do or something we think or define or intellectually master. And Tao escapes that. It transcends that. That's what makes it mystical. That's what makes it religious.

Thomas: So you're defining religion as mysticism now?

Bea: No, I'm not trying to define religion at all. I'm just trying to tell you something about Tao.

Thomas: But you can't do that, remember? "The Tao that can be told is not the true Tao."

Bea: But *that's* a telling.

Thomas: Distinguish! Tao can't be told; but the fact that Tao can't be told, *can* be told.

Bea: And that fact tells you two things about Tao, not just about telling. It tells you what Tao is not and also what Tao is. Do you see that?

Thomas: No. Explain, please.

Bea: What Tao is not is a thing that can be told, defined, objectified in words. Tao is not a word, not a man, not a stone, not a finite, definable anything.

Thomas: Fine. But what about what Tao *is*?

Bea: What Tao *is*, is just Tao.

Thomas: That's an unhelpful tautology, like a glop is a glop.

Bea: No, it has meaning. Tao means "the Way." It's not just an "x," it's a chosen word, one word chosen out of a vocabulary of thousands. It's not a person or a stone or a word, it's a way. And it's *the* way, not just *a* way. *The* way means that it's both unique and universal. It's the way everything is.

Thomas: But that's only an image—like a dirt road or a concrete street—a physical analogy for something that's supposedly not physical.

Bea: That's right. If it was a definition instead of a mere image or analogy, it would contradict that very first point, in the first line: that it can't be told. But you shouldn't say it's *only* an image or an analogy. Analogies are powerful. They're like the starship *Enterprise* in *Star Trek*: they take you "where no one has gone before." They let you understand things you can't understand in any other way.

Thomas: To you, maybe. That one does nothing for me.

Bea: Oh, I forgot, Thomas: your brain has no right hemisphere, you're all left. You're left all alone, you're out in left field, you're left behind.

Thomas: Your analogies are running away with you now and trying to become puns. Can we be literal for a minute about this thing we can't be literal about, this Tao? Can we talk about Tao instead of about me and you?

Bea: Yes, let's try. Let me tell you what intrigues me the most about Taoism, okay?

Thomas: Go ahead.

Bea: It's that in Taoism the Tao, the one Tao, the very same Tao, the one and only Tao, is found in three places, three dimensions, three ontological addresses. First, it's the "way" nature works, and second, it's the "way" the wise man works in imitation of nature. (In fact, it's more often the way the wise *woman* works. But let's let that go for now.) But it's also simply The Way, eternal and absolute. Its other two addresses are in time, but it's also got an eternal address. Tao is eternal. The first line is usually translated, "The Tao that can be told is not the *eternal* Tao."

Thomas: What's your point, Bea? So Tao is eternal, so what?

Bea: But it's also temporal, both in nature and in the life of the sage. The point is that it's the same Tao in all three places.

Thomas: I still don't see what point you're making out of that.

Bea: That it's strikingly similar to the three Western religions there.

Thomas: No it isn't. Tao is not a god. It's not a person, or a creator, or a lawgiver, or a savior.

Bea: But it's like God in being both transcendent and immanent. In both Eastern and Western religions, even though their theology seems so different at first, time is permeated with eternity.

Thomas: Isn't that kind of what you expected to find? Don't all religions say that?

Bea: Yes! That's exactly my point. All religions, however different they are, like Taoism and Christianity, are strikingly similar. They see the same thing: that the whole natural universe and the whole of human life are religious, they're sacred. Because in all religions you see here in time the same Tao that's in eternity, the same Tao that's the absolute, the same Tao that Western religions call "God."

Thomas: Are you reducing the differences between Eastern and Western religions to words now?

Bea: No. There's obviously a big difference. Lao Tzu didn't see Tao as a person. That's what's so impressive: that even despite this big difference, the way Lao Tzu describes the Tao is the way Western religions describe God. To put my point in the terms of Christian trinitarian theology, the divine nature is the same in the two religions even though the divine person or persons are not.

Thomas: Well, in a vague and obvious way, of course it's one and the same: it's just the sense of the sacred, the thing we discussed in the class on primitive religions.

Bea: No, no, it's not an "of course." It's not obvious. It's paradoxical, it's apparently self-contradictory and impossible. How could anything be both temporal and nontemporal?

Thomas: Frankly, Bea, that sounds like nothing more than vague, illogical gibberish to me.

Bea: No, it's not vague, it's very specific. The Tao has a *character*. In fact it has almost all of the attributes of the Western God, point for specific point.

Thomas: That's quite a claim. Prove it.

Bea: Gladly. Let's look at the book, okay? Here, I've marked the things Lao Tzu says about Tao that impressed me when I first read them because they were exactly what I believe about God. The attributes of Taoism's Tao are also attributes of Christianity's God. If you see the same fingerprints on two letters, it shows that it's the same person who wrote them both. And there's forty of those fingerprints.

Thomas: Wait. Before you list them, remember what you're comparing. God is a person. Tao isn't.

Bea: *Three* persons, in Christian theology, but one nature, one substance, one essence. The divine attributes are attributes of the divine nature, which is possessed by all three divine persons in Christianity and one divine person in Judaism and Islam. Lao Tzu didn't know God as a person but he certainly knew a whole lot about the divine nature.

Thomas: That's quite an original claim, Bea.

Bea: Not at all.

Thomas: So who else said that besides you?

Bea: Here's one: an Eastern Orthodox monk who called himself Hieromonk Damascene wrote a book called *Christ the Eternal Tao*, and he claimed to show that no one, not even Aristotle, ever knew more about the divine nature without special religious revelation, by reason alone, than Lao Tzu did in the *Tao Te Ching*. Chinese Bibles for centuries translated the beginning of John's Gospel this way: "In the beginning was the Tao, and the Tao was with God and the Tao was God. . . . And the Tao became flesh and dwelt among us."

Thomas: Very interesting, though it doesn't prove your inclusivism.

Bea: But there's a lot of specific evidence for it in the *Tao Te Ching*. Look at those forty divine attributes in the text.

Thomas: Is that a command or a suggestion? I see you've opened your well-marked copy already. I guess I'm in for a sermon.

Bea: Not a sermon; data.

Thomas: Fine. Show me the data. Show me forty divine attributes. I won't interrupt.

Bea: Okay. Here we go. I'm using Addiss and Lombardo's literal translation of the *Tao Te Ching*.

Number 1: ineffable. Poem 1: "Tao called Tao is not Tao." And poem 56: "Those who know don't talk; those who talk don't know."

Number 2: first cause. Poem 1: "Nameless: the origin of heaven and earth."

Number 3: understood only by a pure heart, not a desiring, grasping will. Poem 1: "Empty of desire, perceive mystery. Filled with desire, perceive manifestations." Here's Jesus' version: "Blessed are the pure of heart, for they shall see God."

Number 4: inexhaustibility. Poem 4: "Tao is empty. Its use never exhausted."

Number 5: infinity. Poem 4: "Bottomless."

Number 6: older than time. Poem 4: "It is older than the Ancestor."

Number 7: active, dynamic. Poem 6: "Endless flow of inexhaustible *energy*."

Number 8: unselfish. Poem 7: "Heaven is long, earth enduring. Long and enduring because they do not exist for themselves. . . . No self-interest? Self is fulfilled."

And the next point is the positive half of this one: Number 9: full of charity, altruism. Poem 8: "Best to be like water, which benefits the ten thousand things."

Number 10: pacifism, nonviolence. Poem 8: "It does not contend."

Number 11: humility. Poem 8: "It pools where humans disdain to dwell."

Number 12: anonymity. Poem 9: "Withdrawing when work is done: Heaven's Tao."

Number 13: independence. Poem 10: "Act without dependence."

Number 14: empty. Not a thing or an object or a substance. Powerful because it's "empty." Poem 11: "Thirty spokes join one hub; the wheel's use comes from emptiness. Clay is fired to make a pot; the pot's use comes from emptiness. Windows and doors are cut to make a room; the room's use comes from emptiness." That's Buddha's metaphysical point about emptiness. The next one is Buddha's moral point about Nirvana:

Number 15: bliss. Poem 13: "The self embodies distress. No self, no distress."

Number 16: love. Poem 13: "Love the world as your self, the world can be your trust." Arthur Waley's translation says, "World rule can be safely entrusted to the man who loves all men as he loves his own body." That's what Saint Paul said about marriage in Ephesians 5: loving your spouse is loving yourself.

Number 17: beyond moral rules and moral virtues and moral feelings, which are a second best. Poem 18: "Great Tao rejected, benevolence and righteousness appear."

Number 18: known intuitively, immediately, wordlessly. Poem 22: "How do I know this? Like this."

Number 19: it gives you life through death, success through failure. Not just pacifism but victory through pacifism. Poem 22: "Sages . . . do not display themselves and therefore shine; do not assert themselves and therefore stand out; do not praise themselves and therefore succeed . . . do not contend and therefore no one under heaven can contend with them." Its secret power is hard softness, or soft hardness. Poem 78: "Nothing in the world is soft and weak as water, but when attacking the hard and strong nothing can conquer so easily. Weak overcomes strong, soft overcomes hard."

Numbers 20 through 28 are all in one poem, poem 25: "Something unformed [infinite] and complete [perfect], before heaven and earth [before time], solitary [unique] and silent [beyond words], stands alone ["the one without a second"] and unchanging [immutable], pervading all things without limit [omnipresent], it is like the mother of all under heaven [giver of life]." That's nine more attributes right there. That makes 28 so far.

Number 28 was motherhood, or source of life. That's in Poem 34 too: "All beings owe their life to it."

Number 29: providence. Poem 34: "It clothes and nourishes all beings but does not become their master."

Number 30: not an object of sight or hearing. Poem 35: "You won't see it, you won't hear it."

Number 31: strong. Poem 43: "The softest thing in the world rides roughshod over the strongest." I guess that's pretty much the same as point 19.

Number 32: kind. Poem 44: "Abuse nothing. . . . Harm nothing."

Number 33: paradoxical. Poem 45: "Great fullness seems empty . . . great straightness seems bent, great skill seems clumsy, great eloquence seems mute."

Number 36: moderate. Poem 46: "Knowing that enough is enough is always enough." That's especially remarkable seeing that it's also *infinite*.

Number 37: nonjudgmental. Poem 51: "People who are good I treat well. People who are not good I also treat well."

Number 38: supernatural. It makes miracles possible. Poem 50: "You have heard of people good at holding on to life. Walking overland they don't avoid rhinos and tigers. In battle they don't arm themselves. The rhino's horn finds nothing to gore, the tiger's claws find nothing to flay, weapons find nothing to pierce."

Number 39: not an object of any outside force or activity. Poem 56: "It can't be embraced, it can't be escaped, it can't be helped, it can't be harmed."

Number 40: the ideal standard even for politics. Poem 60: "Govern big countries as you cook little fish." And poem 61: "A great nation lowers itself and wins over a small one."

Number 41: presence, in fact, omnipresence. Poem 62: "Tao is the mysterious center of all things."

Sorry, I miscalculated. It's 41, not 40. Or maybe it's 40 because two of them were the same. I'm better at religion than at math.

Thomas: It's got to be 41. Isn't 41 the answer to life, the universe, and everything in *The Hitchhiker's Guide to the Galaxy*?

Bea: That was 42, I think.

Thomas: Well, I admit that 41 is quite a list of similarities, even if some of them overlap. But what does it all come down to? Just that the essence of goodness is unselfishness. But Jesus and Buddha said that too. They just weren't as poetic.

Bea: But that's evidence for inclusivism.

Thomas: Moral inclusivism, yes. Moral atheists and agnostics
           like myself, and metaphysicians like Lao Tzu and Plato,
           and nontheistic religious teachers like Buddha, and
           theistic religious teachers like Moses and Jesus all
           preach the same essential morality. But their theologies
           and philosophies still contradict each other. Radically.

Bea: Well, I guess that's another issue for another day. But
           if I admit your case for exclusivism looks strong at
           first on the intellectual level, won't you admit that my
           case for inclusivism is just as strong on the moral level?

Thomas: Yes, but my exclusivism doesn't deny those agreements
           in the moral dimension that you just showed me. But
           your inclusivism does deny any real contradictions in
           the intellectual dimension. So my ism accounts for
           both dimensions of the evidence but yours doesn't.
           My exclusivism is more inclusive than your inclusivism
           because it's inclusive of the data for your inclusivism,
           but your inclusivism doesn't include and explain the
           data for my exclusivism.

Bea: That's very clever, Thomas. But you can't separate those
           two dimensions like that, the practical and the theo-
           retical, or the life view and the world view, or the moral
           and the metaphysical. Because in both religions, Taoism
           and Christianity, I think the two are ultimately identical.
           God *is* love. Moral goodness goes all the way up. God
           is goodness, God *is* the Tao, the life of unselfish love.
           That's the whole point of Taoism—and of Christianity
           too—that goodness is metaphysically real, in fact that
           it's the nature of ultimate reality, that it's the key to
           metaphysics, that the absolute isn't just Truth but
           Goodness, that ethics goes all the way up into

metaphysics. So if religions are inclusive morally, and if theology ultimately *is* morality, a morality way beyond legalism, then theology is inclusivist too.

Thomas: But ethics is about discrimination. There is good and there is evil. But you can't say that there is being *and there is non-being*. All beings are beings. Everything that exists, exists. Metaphysics is just a hypostatization of the law of non-contradiction. But ethics is a series of commandments, or laws, or values, or ideals, or duties. It's specific. It tells you to be this kind of person and live this kind of life rather than the other alternative. There's an alternative to goodness but there's no alternative to being. Ethics is about choices between alternatives. Metaphysics isn't. So—I don't mean to insult you, Bea, but you're just confused when you say ethics goes all the way up into metaphysics. Being has no character, goodness does. Lao Tzu is right about being: being can't be defined. But goodness can.

Bea: But Thomas, don't you see? That's the whole startling point: being *does* have a character. That's Lao Tzu's point and Jesus' point too. Ultimate reality has a personality, a character. And it's the same character in both religions. That's the most startling thing of all: this universal nature of things, the Tao, that exists in all three places, the nature of nature and the nature of God and the nature of the wise person—it's got a character, a personal character, one that's very specific and very surprising. It's selflessness, charity, love, humility, self-giving. It's like a saint, not like a sinner.

Thomas: Sorry, Bea, I just can't see what's so startling about that. You're just hypostatizing an abstraction. You're just putting a metaphysical label on ethics. It's just that we all agree that good people are unselfish. That's all you need to say. You don't need to talk about Tao or God to say that we ought to be good.

Bea: But what goodness looks like is startling. That's the surprise: not just that ethics goes all the way up into metaphysics but that when it does it looks like a saint. Saints are surprising. They're *characters*!

Thomas: I think you have it backwards. The concrete saint looks like that abstract ideal, not vice versa. The saint imitates the Tao, the Tao doesn't imitate a saint.

Bea: You don't understand. It's not an abstraction.

Thomas: What's not an abstraction?

Bea: Tao. It's the nature of reality, the way of reality. It's not just goodness in some vague, generic, ideal sense. It's not just goodness in general, it's a very sharp and striking kind of goodness. It goes beyond obvious, general moral goodness. That's why Lao Tzu says such negative things about ordinary morality: Tao is so much more than that, just as God is more than a set of general moral ideals in Christianity.

Thomas: How is it more?

Bea: Morality is justice and the golden rule. Tao goes beyond justice and beyond the golden rule. It's love, and self-lessness, and humility; it's getting out of the way, a kind of non-busybody charity.

Thomas: I kinda like that. Too much charity is busybody charity, and people who don't want to be busybodies don't do much fussy, busy charity.

Bea: See? You're starting to see it. You're seeing what Tao is and what a saint is.

Thomas: Big deal. I'm not the only one to see that.

Bea: That's my point: all the religions see it. They all say the same surprising thing, this thing that is not obvious or generic. In fact, it's so surprising that it's almost a self-contradiction. You have to lose yourself to find it. Die to live. Self is fulfilled only when self dies.

Thomas: You mean *selfishness* dies, not self. It takes a real self to be unselfish, just as it takes a real self to be selfish.

Bea: Of course.

Thomas: But Buddha disagrees with that. Remember the "no-self" doctrine, *anatta*.

Bea: On the theoretical level, that looks like a contradiction. But not on the practical level. Jesus and Buddha and Lao Tzu all see the same practical point: that fulfillment is emptiness, that it's just the opposite of what you expect it to be. It's not success and getting what you want, and conquest and power, even the power to do good or attain the good. It's *yielding*. That's the paradox, the apparent contradiction: the way is to get out of the way! The self has to be unselfish—that's almost like saying dogs have to be un-doggy, or that circles have to be noncircular. What an amazing thing to say! And all the religions of the world see that and say that. If that's not a proof of inclusivism, I can't imagine what is.

Thomas: Okay, Bea, I admit a lot of the things you say. I admit that unselfishness can seem paradoxical. But it's not surprising. We all know that we ought to be unselfish. And I also admit that it's impressive that so many different teachers teach the same paradox. I admit your ethical universalism. But it's only an ethical paradox, or a psychological paradox. I don't see why you have to make it metaphysical or theological.

Bea: I have to say that because that's the way it is.

Thomas: No, I think you have to say that for another reason. I think you have to say that because if you do, if you unite ethics and metaphysics, then your inclusivism in ethics, which I agree with, flows over into metaphysics and theology too, which I don't agree with. So your tidal wave of inclusion overflows my sea wall of exclusion. It's like the pun Hindus say to Christians: "my karma ran over your dogma." But I say it's the other way around. It's my ism that includes yours. Because my exclusivism doesn't deny that there are a lot of surprising ethical agreements between religions, but your inclusivism denies that there are any real theological disagreements between them. I don't deny your data, but you deny mine. It's *my* karma that runs over *your* dogma.

Bea: Hmph!

Thomas: Is that your answer? Hmph?

Bea: It's not a logical answer, it's a personal disappointment. I'm disappointed in you, Thomas. For a while today you were so affirmative and positive and open minded. You said Taoism made a lot of sense to you. But now you're going back to being negative and skeptical and argumentative again.

Thomas: I'm not negative or skeptical about what you call the character of Tao. I affirm that. That's just what every moral person approves: unselfishness. I'm skeptical about Lao Tzu erecting a metaphysics out of this morality. He seems to think that Tao is a being, a thing, almost a person, something like God. He hypostatizes an abstraction, and then he kind of worships it.

Bea: Taoists don't worship Tao.

Thomas: Oh, I know that. But whether you worship it or not, whether you call it a person—a God—or a force—Tao—that isn't the biggest difference between us. The biggest difference is whether you think it's a real entity outside you, something *like* a God, whether personal or impersonal. It's the difference between Plato and Aristotle. You're a Platonist, I'm an Aristotelian. You worship a supernatural Platonic idea, I just admire a natural Aristotelian form—a form that can be found in some things in nature and in some human lives: the form of goodness. I see no need to go beyond that. I get the same moral force from my Aristotelian natural form as you do from your Platonic supernatural form.

Bea: I don't think you do. And that's my evidence for the real existence of Tao.

Thomas: What evidence?

Bea: It's empirical evidence, it's evidence from our experience. It's like a scientific experiment.

Thomas: What are you talking about? What experience? What experiment?

Bea: The experiment is what Taoists call *wu wei*, or *wei wu wei*: it means "doing without doing," or "acting without acting." It means being receptive, like water, or like a woman's womb. Remember the professor's description of that in class today? It's the practical consequence of the theoretical point, it's the lifestyle of letting Tao into your life, the lifestyle that follows from the metaphysical worldview that Tao really exists. And that's the practical message of all religions, their bottom line, however different their theories are about Tao or God.

Thomas: I know that. So what? What does that prove?

Bea: It's *evidence* for the truth of the metaphysics. Tao is there! You can *experience* Tao if you practice *wu wei*, if you let Tao in, just as a woman can experience pregnancy if she lets a man into her body. A woman getting pregnant is pretty good evidence for the existence of men. And the spiritual pregnancies that you can experience from your *wu wei* toward Tao is pretty good evidence for the existence of Tao. It works. It makes a difference. It makes you different. It empowers you. It gives you *te*, spiritual power. It makes you a better person and it makes your life a better life. It's a "try it, you'll like it" argument.

Thomas: Are you saying you're a better person than I am because you believe your goodness is metaphysical and I don't?

Bea: No . . .

Thomas: Why not? Wouldn't that logically follow from what you just said? You have a God, or a force out there to help you to be good, but I don't. That's got to be an advantage for you.

Bea: Well, sure. But you have that real God outside you too. You just don't believe in him. But my God loves and helps you too, Thomas, not just me. He believes in you even if you don't believe in him.

Thomas: But you have to think of yourself as right and me as wrong.

Bea: Well, of course. That's what it means to have a difference of opinion about anything.

Thomas: But this difference of opinion is about *goodness*. You have to think you have more goodness than I do.

Bea: No I don't. More truth in my thoughts, of course. But not more goodness in my life, or my character.

Thomas: But there's got to be at least a connection between those two. If you have the right road map about the land of goodness, and I don't, then that has to have consequences. And one of those consequences has to be that you can be more of a saint than I am, because I think saintliness is just a human ideal and you think it's an absolute reality. The mind and the will have to be connected, right? So a better mind—yours, if you're right—has to result in a better will—yours. So even though you don't *want* to claim personal moral superiority over me, you logically have to, if you claim intellectual superiority.

Bea: No I don't.

Thomas: Why not? I just proved that you have to. What's the fallacy in my proof?

Bea: Even if I *can* be more of a saint than you can because of my religion, that doesn't mean that I am. Even if my religion gives me more resources, that doesn't mean that I've taken advantage of them. You've only got a fiddle and I've got a Stradivarius, but maybe you're playing better music than I am because you're trying harder.

Thomas: Oh. Okay. But we've drifted away from Taoism into ourselves, as usual.

Bea: Oops. We have, haven't we? Hey, maybe that's the universal essence of religion. I mean: doing the opposite of that.

Thomas: We'll have to ask the professor about that next time. Hey, I didn't even notice: he didn't come today. I hope he's not sick.

Bea: It's probably another one of those committee meetings. And he *is* sick—he's sick of them.

Thomas: Are you getting sick of our dialogue?

Bea: No, not sick of it, not at all, just kind of tired. Let's leave it for now, as long as we can still part as friends, okay?

Thomas: Okay. Even though we didn't succeed in any breakthroughs or agreements yet. We're as far apart as we ever were.

Bea: Oh, I think we did succeed. Because I think a union of two people in friendship is a lot more of a success than a union of two minds in an idea. Don't you?

Thomas: I'll have to think about that, Bea. I really will. Because I think maybe that's the best thing you've said yet. The thing *I* most needed to learn, anyway.

8

JUDAISM

Human Culture or Divine Revelation?

Thomas: Well, Bea, what did you learn from that lecture?

Bea: Hmm. . . . I was about to answer, "Not much," because I was already pretty familiar with Judaism—much more than with any of the other religions we've covered so far. But then I suddenly realized that this course isn't so much about knowing historical facts as it is about philosophical perspectives, and in that sense I learned a lot.

Thomas: What do you mean by "philosophical perspectives"?

Bea: I think the professor's main aim is not just filling our heads with knowledge so that we can get As on tests but inveigling us to look at the different religions of the world differently, to cock our heads to the side, so to speak. It's about looking *along* each religion instead of just looking *at* it, as you'd look along a sign, or a word, rather than just at it, as you'd look at a rock.

Thomas: I think you're right there, Bea. That's a good way to put it. So . . . interpreting my question that way, let me ask it again: what did you learn?

Bea: The first thing that pops into my mind when I think of the Jews is something I find disturbing.

Thomas: Good! That means you're philosophizing. What is it?

Bea: Their exclusivism. Both as a people and as a religious belief system. No people has kept their own distinctive identity as the Jews have. Maybe that's the explanation for anti-Semitism: jealousy. The Jews are like a stone in the world's stomach. It can't digest them and it can't ignore them.

Thomas: That's true. No people has resisted assimilation as much as they have. And no people has been less ecumenical toward other religions. They have the longest track record in history of refusing to believe other religions, refusing to worship other people's gods. Their scriptures are full of God condemning that, more repeatedly and consistently than he condemns anything else. And even Jesus bought into that: he took the first of the Ten Commandments and called it the greatest one of all: "Thou shalt have no other gods." And the Muslims have bought into it too: "No god but God." That's their primary prayer, the shahada.

So it looks like you've got a double problem there, Bea. First, as a Christian, you can't disagree with Jesus, and second, since Jesus was a Jew, you can't disagree with his Judaism, no matter how exclusivistic it seems. Not only can't you be anti-Jewish, you have to be anti-Gentile. The Jews are right and everybody else is wrong wherever they contradict the Jews.

Bea: No, I don't have to be anti-Gentile. Jesus opened the door to all the Gentiles.

Thomas: Well, in a sense that's historically true. That's why Christians send out missionaries but Jews don't. The Jews are still waiting for the Messiah. They believe that only when the Messiah comes will the whole world worship the true God.

Bea: But half the world does worship the true God now, the God of the Jews, and that's because the Messiah did come, and he broke down the wall of separation between Jews and Gentiles. That's inclusivism, not exclusivism.

Thomas: No, you've still got a wall of exclusivism, it's just bigger. It surrounds not just Jews but Jews, Christians, and Muslims, who all worship the God of the Jews. The other half of the world is still wrong if they don't worship the God of the Jews. Jesus didn't abrogate the first commandment. He repeated it.

Bea: There's nothing in the Bible, Old Testament or New, about any other world religion except polytheism, worshiping many gods. That's condemned, that's excluded, yes. But that's pretty much dead today. All the major world religions are monotheistic. They agree with Jewish monotheism, even though they have very different perspectives on this one God.

Thomas: But some don't even use the word *God*.

Bea: So what? A God by any other name—or none—would smell as sweet.

Thomas: Look what we're doing again. Our class was about Judaism, not inclusivism versus exclusivism. Let's talk about Judaism today. We'll talk about comparative religions later. We agreed that we should get all our data straight first before we claim to compare them.

Bea: Okay. What do you want to talk about?

Thomas: Something we can sink our teeth into and argue about.

Bea: Okay, how about the explanation for the Jews' incredible achievements in history? Remember the professor's quotation—I forget where it was from—that the Jews refute every major law of history. Everybody wants to kill them, from Pharaoh to Hitler, yet they've survived for 3,500 years. And they thrive. They're one of the smallest religions in the world—what is it, less than one percent of the world?—yet half the world now believes in their God. And it's a lot more likely that a doctor, lawyer, scientist, artist, comedian, novelist, publisher, musician, philosopher, or banker is a Jew than anything else. What's the cause for that?

Thomas: They have an answer: they're God's "chosen people." But you can't believe that if you're an inclusivist, right?

Bea: No, I don't think that necessarily follows. Because they don't mean by that that they're better than anybody else. Their scriptures explicitly say that. God tells them why he chose them: not because they were wiser or stronger or better—in fact he calls them "a stiff-necked people"—but just because he loved them. It's the humblest interpretation they could possibly put on the data of their miraculous successes. It's God's doing, not theirs.

Thomas: Yet they're still different, even if that's God's doing, not theirs. So it's God who's the exclusivist.

Bea: I don't know what to say to that.

Fesser: (approaching) Did I just hear a bit of Socratic humility from one of you?

Bea: That was me, Professor.

Thomas: I thought I was the Socratic one.

Bea: But I'm the humble one.

Thomas: And proud of it too, I see.

Fesser: I see nothing has changed in my absence: you're still in each other's hair. Sorry to be late again for our little informal class. So tell me, did you solve the problem we raised in class about whether Judaism is primarily a race, a culture, or a religion? Or about the problem of a special divine revelation to them—what theologians call "the scandal of particularity"?

Thomas: "How odd / of God / to choose / the Jews"—Hilaire Belloc, right?

Fesser: Yes. Although he didn't mean it to be as anti-Semitic as it sounds.

Thomas: No, we didn't solve those questions because we didn't raise them yet.

Bea: So let's raise them now.

Thomas: Okay, let's start with the professor's question about whether Judaism is primarily a race, a culture, or a religion.

Bea: Well, Judaism can't be primarily a racial thing because that would make them racists, right?

Thomas: I think you can guess what my next question is going to be, Bea.

Bea: Um, define my terms, right? Okay, racism is the erroneous idea that your biological race is . . . is terribly, terribly important. And that yours is extra special.

Thomas: Well, I guess that makes me a racist.

Bea: What? I'm shocked. Why?

Thomas: Because race is nothing but an extension of family. Both are based on the biology of reproduction, on "blood," if you will. And family is terribly important, isn't it? Isn't "extra special" loyalty and love to your family very important and very right?

Bea: I never thought of it that way.

Thomas: And isn't culture and cultural tradition an aspect of this extended family called race? Or, to put it the other way, isn't race an aspect of culture?

Bea: I guess so.

Thomas: And that's why tradition is so important for Jews. It's "all in the family"—family memories. It's their past, their roots, that gives them their identity.

Bea: True. But Gentiles can become Jews too—proselytes.

Thomas: Yes, but that's the exception that proves the rule. It's like adoption. It doesn't change the essence of a family. Conversion to Judaism is like adoption: it's a legitimate door, but it's a back door, not the front door. The front door is procreation, reproduction. That's something racial.

Fesser: So, Thomas, you're reducing the three options to two then, in answering our question about race, culture, or religion. You're saying that Judaism is essentially either a racial and cultural thing or a religious thing. Is that what you're saying?

Thomas: I guess so. I'm saying that it's either natural or supernatural, since both race and culture are natural and religion—at least biblical Judaism—is supernatural.

Fesser: In that case, you're asking which person is *not* a Jew: the racial and cultural Jew who doesn't believe the Jewish religion, or the Gentile who does.

Thomas: I guess so.

Fesser: But Christians fit that second category, don't they? Isn't that what Saint Paul said in the New Testament?

You're a child of Abraham not by being circumcised in your body but in your soul, in your heart. So according to Christianity, Christians are really Jews even if they're not racially Jewish because Judaism is essentially religious, and Christians believe the religion of the Jews. But Jews don't call Christians a certain kind of Jew just because they believe Jewish theology and morality. The *Jewish* definition of a Jew is racial: a Jew is someone who has a Jewish mother. And even religiously, it's circumcision that initiates you into the religion, into the covenant with God, because God himself invented that covenant and that way of initiation into it.

Thomas: Right.

Fesser: And even if a Jew defines Judaism religiously, his definition of a Jew isn't like the Christian definition of a Christian: it's not whether you believe the theology and the morality. It's whether you practice it, whether you observe the Law. It's works, not faith. But according to the New Testament, Christianity is first of all faith.

Thomas: Okay. So that question about what makes a Jew a Jew, according to Judaism, is answered. So what? How is that important for the larger question we keep coming back to, the question of comparative religions?

Fesser: I think the answer is that when you compare Judaism with Christianity, you're comparing apples with oranges. They're two different kinds of isms. They self-define differently.

Thomas: Right. So how does that help our debate between exclusivism and inclusivism?

Fesser: It makes both of those isms wrong.

Thomas: So pluralism is the only option left.

Fesser: *Quod erat demonstrandum.*

Thomas: But Judaism and Christianity contradict each other. You can't be a Jew if you accept Jesus as the Son of God and the Messiah. So they're still exclusive, from the Jewish point of view anyway.

Fesser: Yes, that's the sticking point.

Bea: So exclusivism raises its ugly head again.

Fesser: Yes, but so does inclusivism. If a mystic heard what we said today, he wouldn't be convinced he was wrong either.

Bea: So all three isms are still on the table.

Fesser: Oh, of course they are. I didn't mean to take any of them off it. I just meant to put pluralism on the table too. Because that's the third option that neither of you were considering.

Bea: Professor, I'm still not clear about the answer to our original question about what kind of thing Judaism is. Is it essentially a culture that contains a religion or a religion that contains a culture?

Fesser: You would get different answers to that question from different Jews. So I can't give you a definitive answer. But I can give you another question: why do you think that question is important, and not just for Jews?

Thomas: (interrupting) Because if it's essentially a religion, it makes absolute claims, and if it's a culture, it doesn't.

Fesser: Yes, that's a big difference philosophically. And why is that important religiously?

Thomas: Because if it's a religion, it's claiming a divine revelation, a way down from God, something that's infallible, if God is infallible. If not, not.

Fesser: What would you say if I challenged the implied premise of your argument: that all religions claim a divine revelation? Do Buddhism and Confucianism claim divine revelation?

Thomas: No. They're ways up, not ways down. But religious Jews do claim a divine revelation, a way down, don't they?

Fesser: Yes. And nonreligious Jews don't. They just claim a good and wise human tradition: something horizontal, not necessarily vertical.

Bea: But nonreligious Jews often still respect and practice parts of the Jewish religion. I know quite a few like that. They don't deny the whole vertical dimension. They're not all atheists.

Fesser: Yes, but insofar as they do believe in a "vertical," insofar as they do reach up toward the divine, they see it as man's fallible search for God, not God's infallible revelation to man, as the Orthodox do.

Thomas: So non-Orthodox Jews would say that that's all Judaism is? Even the Law? Even the Ten Commandments?

Fesser: I think most Reform Jews would say that. And some Conservative Jews would, but I think most would not. And no Orthodox Jews would say that.

Thomas: That's an important difference.

Fesser: Why do you think it's important?

Thomas: Because it impacts the issue of comparative religions. Reform Jews can be inclusivists, but Orthodox Jews have to be exclusivists, I think.

Fesser: Why do you think they have to be exclusivists?

Thomas: Because they can't put their divine revelation on par with other religions if those other religions are merely human roads up the mountain. All human roads may be the same, or equal in value, but no human road up can be equal to a divine road down, if that's what they believe Judaism is.

Bea: Why couldn't there be many divine roads down?

Thomas: Because God never contradicts himself, and Judaism contradicts other religions. It did from the beginning, when God supposedly chose them and separated them from all the other tribes and told them not to worship any other gods. Jews were the least inclusive people in the world. That's why the Romans persecuted them: not because the Romans wouldn't tolerate the Jewish religion but because the Jews wouldn't tolerate the Roman religion. They wouldn't be ecumenical and inclusive and tolerant and "just live and let live" and worship Caesar as well as their own god, as all the other religions did. They were like the early Christians that way, and that's why they and the early Christians were the only ones the Romans persecuted: because they were exclusivists. Isn't that right, Professor?

Fesser: Yes; as far as I know those were the only two religions Rome did not tolerate. Politically, the Romans persecuted anyone who wouldn't swear allegiance to Caesar, whether the motive was religious or not. Rome's real religion was Rome.

Bea: But that doesn't prove whether exclusivism or inclusivism is *true*.

Thomas: Of course not. But it shows the inconsistency of your position, Bea. You're a Christian, yet you're an inclusivist. You would have burned incense to Caesar if you had to, and all the other early Christians would have called you an apostate for being an inclusivist. That proves that you can't be a Christian and an inclusivist.

Bea: It proves no such thing.

Thomas: Why not?

Bea: Because if you look at the inner content of these two religions instead of the attitude that Rome took to them, you see that what's distinctive about religious Judaism, as well as the Christianity that came from it, was its inclusivism, its universalism. Look at the main distinctive religious ideas in Judaism: they're all inclusivist, universalist ideas. There's only one God for the whole world, not many. And this God created the whole world and all people. They're all his children, made in his image. And this God is the final end of all people too: there's only one heaven for everybody. And this God revealed the Ten Commandments for everybody, not just for the Jews, although their ceremonial laws and their civil laws are just for them. And this God demands personal holiness and personal justice of every individual, Gentile as well as Jew. That's—what? Five? Six?

Thomas: Five.

Bea: Five distinctively Jewish religious ideas. And they're all universalist ideas. They're "the chosen people" only because they're chosen to remind the whole world of the one universal truth.

Thomas: But other religions deny that universal truth.

Bea: No, they don't; they just have different versions of it.

Thomas: Okay, here are three examples. We went over a dozen more before, but let me just repeat three of them. Number one: Hindus and some Buddhists worship many gods. Number two: they don't believe that God created the universe out of nothing. Number three: they don't believe that God is a person with a will who gives moral commandments.

Fesser: Good choice, Thomas. Those are three of the main ideas that apparently separate Judaism from Eastern religions. What do you make of them, Bea? How do you see them as not contradicting Eastern religions?

Bea: The first one is easy. All religions are monotheistic. The many gods are just masks for the One. And the second one is just technical. All religions see the One as the source of the many; they just use different images for it. The West uses the image of a craftsman or an artist making things outside of himself, and the East uses the image of a dreamer dreaming things inside himself. And the third one—what was your third one, Thomas?

Thomas: Moral commandments.

Bea: Oh, yes. That's the easiest one of all: all religions have the same moral laws. Morality is the strongest case for inclusivism. It's much more obviously the same across different religions than theology is.

Thomas: But it doesn't come from God in Eastern religions.

Bea: But even Eastern religions don't *deny* that it comes from God. They're not atheistic about God, they're just agnostic.

Thomas: But they say God is not a person with a moral will, so morality doesn't go "all the way up."

Bea: In a sense it *does*, because it's absolute, so it's grounded in the one absolute, however you conceive that absolute: He, She, It, or Them. It's just that the theological images for the absolute are different in the East. They're less personal.

Thomas: Well, why isn't *that* a contradiction to Western theology?

Bea: Because in Western theology, too, God is not *just* a person, or three persons, but also a single divine nature or substance or essence or however they label it. We have to have some image in our mind to understand him, so in the Bible he's imaged as a kind of supernatural person. The East doesn't use that image. But that's not a contradiction, because different images don't exclude each other, as two contradictory *ideas* do. They can complement each other. I don't need to be an inclusivist about imagery; I don't need to insist that everyone use the same image for God. I'm an inclusivist only about the substance, the essence. And the substance transcends the images. *Both* sides say that, by the way: that what God really is transcends all of our images. That's why Western religions are forbidden to make or worship images. And I take that to mean word images as well as "graven images."

Fesser: That's a good defense of inclusivism, Bea. And you have a strong argument for exclusivism, Thomas.

Thomas: And that's why you choose pluralism? Because both of us have equally good arguments?

Fesser: That can be one reason, yes.

Thomas: I still think my arguments outweigh yours, Bea.

Bea: Why?

Thomas: Because I've made a positive case; all you've done is defend your inclusivism against it. You haven't proved your side positively.

Bea: So go read Frithjof Schuon's *The Transcendent Unity of Religions*, or Aldous Huxley's *The Perennial Philosophy*.

Thomas: But religious Jews have always been exclusivists, throughout their history, as Hindus have always been religious inclusivists. There's certainly a contradiction *there*. You can't be inclusivist about inclusivism versus exclusivism. And since Hinduism is inclusivism and

Judaism is exclusivism, you can't be inclusivist about Judaism and Hinduism, or Judaism and Buddhism.

Bea: By the way, I know quite a few Jews who are very interested in Buddhism. I wonder why that is.

Thomas: Oh, I've got an answer to that. Jews have to take the commandments very seriously because they're God's commandments. And they're commanded: love your neighbor as yourself. And that's hard to do. Buddhism tells us that there is no self! So it lets us off the hook.

Bea: Are you serious?

Thomas: Of course not. That's a Jewish joke.

Bea: Oh.

Thomas: But back to our point: Jews aren't inclusive to Gentiles, even though Gentiles might be inclusive to Jews. Religiously, I mean. Take Jews and Hindus. Hindus are inclusive to Jews—they'd probably classify Judaism as another yoga path up the one mountain—but Jews aren't inclusive to Hindus. They're not part of the covenant. They're uncircumcised.

Bea: You're arguing about attitudes to people now, Thomas. That's psychology, not theology.

Thomas: Fine. Let's argue about theology. Hindus see Judaism as another form of Hinduism, but Jews don't see Hinduism as another form of Judaism. So whoever's right there, whether the Hindu inclusivists or the Jewish exclusivists, they contradict each other. Whether or not exclusivism is true between Jews and Hindus, it's certainly true between exclusivists and inclusivists. And since Jews are exclusivists and Hindus are inclusivists, exclusivism is true between Jews and Hindus. Unless the law of non-contradiction is untrue. And if that's untrue, then we *can* contradict ourselves, so we can say that if it's untrue, then it's true. So it's true either way.

Bea: That's very clever, Thomas, but it's not religion. You sound like a very clever kid using a computer.

Thomas: A minute ago you complained that my argument was psychology instead of logic, and now you complain that it's logic instead of psychology. No matter what I say, I can't please you. Is that a woman's privilege?

Bea: So now we're getting sexist and chauvinistic!

Fesser: Uh—hey, troops, we're supposed to be all on the same side, fighting ignorance instead of each other. Can we get back to the issues instead of the personal insults?

a and Thomas: Sorry.

Thomas: Bea, let me ask a question that's both logical and personal. That's okay, right? Because you'd say your inclusivism is both a philosophy and a personal attitude, right?

Bea: Right.

Thomas: So my question is this: As a Christian, how far does your inclusivism extend? To Jews, of course, because Jesus was a Jew. And to Hinduism too, right? And all the religions of the world in some way?

Bea: Yes, exactly: "in some way."

Thomas: What about Satanism, then? In what way do you as a worshiper of Christ accept the religion that worships the antichrist?

Bea: No, of course I have to draw the line there.

Thomas: So you do draw lines.

Bea: Of course.

Thomas: So you are an exclusivist, then. You're just not as narrow an exclusivist as I am.

Bea: You could put it that way, I guess.

Thomas: So the only question that divides us then is not whether you draw lines, but where? And why?

Bea: I'm sure there's a good answer to that question, Thomas. But I'm not sure I could give it to you on the spot. I'll have to think more about that.

Thomas: That was what I said at the end of last week's conversation. Maybe we're both learning Socrates's "lesson one," that we both know less than we think we do. What do you think about that, Professor?

Fesser: I think that you two are both really good teachers to each other. Because you both make each other think. And that's the main purpose of a good teacher. So I think that therefore maybe you don't need me as much as you think you do.

Bea: Well, maybe today, anyway. We seem to be all talked out for today, even though we didn't convince each other. Probably we never will.

Fesser: And that fact might be another good argument for pluralism.

Thomas: You're *assuming* it's a fact that we never will, Professor. But I'm not convinced it is.

Fesser: Good for you, Thomas. "Question authority," especially the authority of professors.

9

ISLAM

Is Surrender Fundamentalism or the Heart of Religion?

Bea: Well, Thomas, I guess you enjoyed that class.

Thomas: Why? Do you think I'm closer to being a Muslim than anything else?

Bea: No, but I think you admire Muslim exclusivism.

Thomas: Actually, Bea, this class brought me closer to your inclusivism than any other class did.

Bea: Oh. That's a surprise. But I think I can guess why. It's because you found yourself less in sympathy with Islam than with any other religion, right? And with its exclusivism, which is very far from your agnosticism? So it had a kind of rebound effect on you?

Thomas: No, just the opposite: because I think this class presented something pretty close to the heart of all religion, which would be an argument for inclusivism, for a religious universal.

Bea: That's a big surprise. What's that universal?

Thomas: Islam, of course.

Bea: What? Why do you pick *that* religion as the universal essence of *all* religions? It's the most exclusivistic and polemical of them all.

Thomas: No, not Islam the religion, Islam the practice: surrender, submission, the peace, the *shalom*, that comes from yielding the human will to the divine will.

Bea: How can that be the universal essence of all religion? Most Eastern religions don't even have a God with a will to surrender to.

Thomas: It's not the theology of God that's universal, it's the surrender to it.

Bea: To "it" or to "him"?

Thomas: To some sort of "higher power," however variously conceived. By the way, there are three examples of Eastern religions that *do* have a God with a will.

Bea: Three?

Thomas: Yes. Ramanuja's Hinduism and its bhakti yoga is one. Pure Land Buddhism is a second. And the "will of heaven" in Confucianism is a third. And certainly Taoism is big on surrender to Tao, even though Tao isn't a personal God with a will.

Bea: So you're an inclusivist now?

Thomas: Not at all. There are still contradictions. But there's also an impressive agreement.

Bea: But it's only on the human side, the psychological side, right? All religions agree in teaching surrender to a "higher power," but you still say they don't agree about that "higher power," right?

Thomas: Look at what's happened to us, Bea: you're arguing for exclusivism and I'm arguing for inclusivism!

Bea: Yes. Look what happens when you look.

Thomas: You could almost say that the first half of the shahada is what all the great religions agree on: that "there is no God but God." They're all monotheistic.

Bea: Except for polytheistic levels of Hinduism and Buddhism. They do mention many gods, after all.

Thomas: But the great gurus say they're all masks for the One.

Bea: Okay, but the second half of the shahada is proper to Islam alone: that Muhammad is the final prophet. If you believe that, you believe that Muhammad's Qur'an is the final divine revelation and everything else is judged by that standard and found wanting in some way, right?

Thomas: So now you see the point of exclusivism.

Bea: As you see the point of inclusivism.

Thomas: I sense that you're not quite convinced, even though you see the point.

Bea: And I sense the same thing about you. We've just stepped into each other's shoes, but we still have our own feet.

Thomas: That's a pretty good way of putting it, Bea.

Bea: You know, one of the greatest of all inclusivists, Frithjof Schuon, was a Muslim, a Sufi. They're much more inclusivist than Sunni or Shiite Muslims. He did the same thing, from the Western side, that Radhakrishnan did from the Eastern side, from Hinduism: he actually practiced each world religion, not just externally but internally, in his life and his experience. And both came up with the same conclusion from their experience: that all religions were true.

Thomas: I don't doubt their sincerity or their intelligence, but I just can't see how they can say that. That's why I'm an exclusivist. What do they do with the contradictions?

Bea: Which ones?

Thomas: The big ones, the ones that separate the West from the East. Is it theist creationism or pantheism? And within the East, is it the Hindu Brahman and Atman or the Buddhist "no-Atman"? And within the West, is it Jewish and Muslim unitarianism or Christian trinitarianism? Is Jesus the Son of God or not? And is Moses or Jesus or Muhammad the definitive prophet?

Bea: All of the above.

Thomas: You can *say* it but that doesn't *explain* it. Start with the first point: does God have a will and did he create the world, or is God just mind and is the world just his dream? How can a Muslim also be a Hindu?

Bea: Sikhs are. They're both. They combine Islam and Hinduism.

Thomas: I don't see how. Can you explain that?

Bea: I'm afraid I know very little about the Sikhs, so I couldn't give you the details. But I can give you the principles of inclusivism in general.

Thomas: I've heard them already, Bea. From you, in fact. What surprises me today is our role reversal: you're arguing for at least something in exclusivism—and I'm thinking that's because you see some truth in it—and I'm arguing for a little bit of inclusivism, because maybe I'm seeing some truth in it. I think we're both testing our new insights against each other.

Bea: Yes, I think we both are. And that's wonderful. You surprise me, Thomas. I thought you'd use Islam to argue for the most absolute exclusivism and say they worshiped a different God, Allah, instead of Jehovah or Jesus. And that would explain the passion of religious wars between Muslims and both Jews and

Christians throughout history. Exclusive absolutes motivate absolute exclusions.

Thomas: Maybe that's right about history. Maybe that perception on both sides—that two different Western religions were worshiping two different Gods—was the cause of the religious wars and of their total passion. But it's clearly a mistake.

Bea: So now you're saying that exclusivism is a mistake?

Thomas: No, no, just that the perception that Allah is a different God than the God of the Jews and the Christians. There are still contradictions, but not about the quantity or the quality of God. Muslims, Jews, and Christians agree that God is only one and that he has every one of the ninety-nine attributes mentioned in the Qur'an. They're all in the Torah and the New Testament too, and also the hundredth one, the one that can't be put into words. It's clearly the same God all three religions worship, and clearly for all three religions worship means total surrender.

Bea: Okay, let's continue this role playing, then. You're defending a little bit of inclusivism and I'm defending the arguments for exclusivism, at least as a thought experiment, and you should try to answer my arguments with a little bit of inclusivism, as you see it. So let's play that serious game and see who wins.

Thomas: Okay, but what we want to see is which position wins, not which person.

Bea: Right. Go ahead, then, refute the idea that the three Western religions don't worship the same God.

Thomas: Okay. I refuted it already by their common description of the attributes of the one God. But here's another reason, a historical reason. The three Abrahamic

religions can't worship three different Gods because
they all worship the God of Abraham. Christians and
Muslims both learned who God was from the same
source, from the Jews.

Bea: But Muslims don't accept the scriptures of the Jews
and of the Christians. They say they are later corrup-
tions, and that's why they contradict the Qur'an and
the Qur'an corrects them. And that's why there are
contradictions between these religions about things
that aren't accidental or negotiable, according to exclusivists. There are important disagreements as well
as important agreements.

Thomas: Right. But the agreements are more important than
the disagreements. Muslims call Jews and Christians
"people of the Book" and say that their scriptures, even
with their mistakes, reveal the same God, so that all
three religions worship the same God, even though
they have three different names for him. The Qur'an
even calls good Jews and Christians "surrenderers"
or Muslims.

Bea: But fundamentalists in all three religions don't agree
with that. They argue that the other two religions are
worshiping a different God. For instance, Christian
fundamentalists say that Muslims are worshiping a
different God because Muslims deny the Trinity and
the divinity of Christ. They say that the God who is
not a Trinity, but only one person, is a different God
than the God who *is*, and that the God who has no
Son is not the same God as the God who has a Son.
In fact the Qur'an calls Christianity a horrible blas-
phemy for saying that God has a Son. What do you
do with that?

Thomas: That's easy, if you know a little logic. There's a logical fallacy in that argument. If I vote for a certain candidate because I believe he never lies, and you vote for the same candidate because you think he does lie sometimes, we still vote for the same candidate even though one of us is wrong about one of his attributes. If fundamentalists argue that Muslims are worshiping a different God than Christians do just because they deny that God has a Son, then Jews are worshiping a different God than Christians do too, because they too don't believe that God has a Son. But no Christian can say that, because Jesus was a Jew, and in all his criticisms of his fellow Jews he never once said that the God of their religion was not the true God, or that he was starting a new religion with a different God. In fact, he said just the opposite: "I came not to destroy the law and the prophets, but to fulfill them." In fact, if you worship a different God just because you differ about one of his attributes, then even Eastern Orthodox Christians and Roman Catholic Christians don't worship the same God because they differ about whether the Holy Spirit proceeds from the Father alone—that's Eastern Orthodox theology—or from the Father and the Son together—that's Roman Catholic theology. That's absurd. So we have a logical reductio ad absurdum argument that disproves the premise that the different religions worship different Gods by showing that that premise logically entails an absurd conclusion.

Bea: So you've just disproved fundamentalist theology. Good for you.

Fesser: (suddenly arriving, late as usual) I heard most of that argument, Thomas. And I think it's a good one. But I don't think Bea's term for it is the right one.

Thomas: *Fundamentalism*, you mean?

Fesser: Yes.

Thomas: Why? Is it because most people who use that term mean something very vague and subjective by it—any closed-minded, narrow-minded attitude—instead of something clear and theological?

Fesser: Well, that too, yes, but also because it's a particular term and it can't be used for a universal critique. It's a Christian term. It arose in the early twentieth century as a protest against liberal or modernist theologians who called themselves Christians but didn't believe in the supernatural or miracles, and it meant belief in five "fundamentals" of the Christian faith, all of which were miraculous and supernatural, especially the literal resurrection of Jesus. So to speak of Muslims as "fundamentalists" is like speaking of Christians as Sunnis or Shiites.

Thomas: I see. You're arguing for pluralism.

Fesser: Yes. Because each religion is so different that it's unfair to use its terms to describe and critique other religions, just as it's unfair for men to call women "soft men" or for women to call men "hard women."

Thomas: So we can't say whether the different religions are compatible, as inclusivists say, or incompatible, as exclusivists say, because we have no terms or standards to compare them that don't come from one of those religions, and therefore prejudge the issue.

Fesser: Yes, that's my argument.

Thomas: But there *are* universal standards: the standards of logic. The law of non-contradiction isn't particular to any one religion.

Fesser: No, it isn't. But it isn't a religious idea either. Shouldn't we compare and judge religions by religious standards?

Thomas: I guess we have to.

Fesser: But if we do, we have no neutral standards; we have to choose the standards of some particular religion—just as we did in that bad argument from the fundamentalists that supposedly proved exclusivism by arguing that Muslims and Christians worshiped different Gods.

Thomas: Hmm. . . . I think I *was* wrong when I agreed to your premise, Professor: that we have to judge religions by religious standards.

Fesser: Why? Because that premise would entail the pluralist conclusion? If that's your argument, then you're *assuming* that pluralism is wrong instead of *proving* it.

Thomas: No, that's not my reasoning. That would be using a religious premise—that pluralism is the right relation between religions. I'm not using a religious premise at all, just a logical one. And I think we have to do that because nonreligious premises are the only ones that everybody shares, so they're the only fair ones to apply to religious dialogue. Both teams in any game have to share a common playing field and common rules. Whenever you argue with someone else, the two of you have to share a common premise if you want to lead the other person to your conclusion. That's a basic principle of logical argument.

Bea: But there *is* a common *religious* premise, not just a common logical premise.

Thomas: That's the claim of inclusivism. But you haven't proved that, and you haven't defined just what that common religious premise is. Remember the first day of class? We didn't even answer the professor's very first question—to define what the word *religion* means in a way that's universal and acceptable to everybody in all religions.

Fesser: I agree with you here, Thomas. Bea, you inclusivists may indeed find a common religious *something*, if your mystics are right, but it's not a definition of religion that everyone accepts, or a starting point or a premise for interreligious dialogue. It's a conclusion. And it's a conclusion not everyone accepts. And it's a conclusion not of logical argument but of mystical experience.

Thomas: Sorry, Bea, today it's two to one. You lose.

Fesser: Not so fast, Thomas. You're assuming that if inclusivism fails, exclusivism wins. That's an exclusivist premise. So that too is not a conclusion but a premise, a controversial premise, and we pluralists deny that premise, that either/or premise that it's either inclusivism or exclusivism, so that if inclusivism is false, exclusivism has got to be true. There's a third position that denies the either/or premise, and that's pluralism.

Thomas: So if you're right, we're right back where we started. We haven't made any progress at all.

Fesser: Come, now, Thomas, you know better than that. Did Socrates make no progress at all in the first half of his dialogues where all he did was to refute his opponents' simple certainties? Even when the dialogue ended with uncertainty, which the early dialogues often do (like the *Meno*), was nothing accomplished? Should he have aborted the questioning?

Thomas: No. They made progress in understanding. The arguments led somewhere.

Fesser: So let's keep following the arguments. If you're on a new and unknown river, if you let the river carry your boat, you never can tell where the trip will take you until you actually take it, right?

ɔmas and Bea: Right.

Fesser: So let's see where the next class leads us.

CHRISTIANITY

The Most Believed (and Most Unbelievable) Claim Ever Made

Fesser: Hello, troops. Ready for another skirmish today?

Bea: Oh. Hi, Professor. We're the late ones this time. How long have you been sitting on that bench waiting for us?

Fesser: Only a minute or two. But let me test you with an alternative answer. What religion would I be believing if I answered: "I've been waiting about 13.7 billion years"?

Bea: It would have to be either Judaism or Christianity.

Fesser: Why?

Bea: Because if you were there 13.7 billion years ago, you would have to be God the Big Banger who created time in the Big Bang, right?

Fesser: Thomas, do you agree with that?

Thomas: No.

Fesser: Why not?

Thomas: Because Christians (with some exceptions) don't believe they're God. But Hindus do. So you'd be a *Hindu* if you

said that. But since your *real* answer to our question
was "only a minute or two," you're not a Hindu.

Bea: Why can't he be both a Hindu and a Christian?

Thomas: Because his two answers about time contradict each
other. He can't be here only a few minutes and also
13 billion years.

Bea: Yes, he can, if the infinite can include the finite, and
eternity can include time. If we're both Brahman and
our human egos, then we're both eternal and temporal.

Thomas: So you're both human and divine, like Jesus.

Bea: Yes!

Thomas: So now you're saying that we're all Jesus. Is that what
Christians believe?

Bea: In a sense . . .

Thomas: So you're one of the three persons of the Trinity?
Christians call Jesus "the *only* begotten Son of God"
in their creeds. So if you're that one, and the only one,
what does that make me? Should I worship you?

Bea: That's not what I meant.

Thomas: So what *did* you mean when you said that we're all
Jesus in a sense? Define your terms!

Bea: I don't like your little logic games, Thomas. You're not
trying to learn anything positive, you're just trying to
tear apart everything I say. That's a cheap and easy
game. Your little logic game is your god.

Thomas: But Bea, logic isn't *mine*. And it's not "little." And it's
not a "game." And it's not a god to me. Nothing is.

Bea: What is logic to you, then?

Thomas: It's the way things are.

Bea: Not to the mystics, it's not.

Thomas: Oh, so now you're a mystic? A minute ago you were Jesus.

Fesser: Excuse me, but I need to interrupt both of you.

Bea: I appreciate your interruption, Professor.

Fesser: Can we all look at our subject instead of at each other? This class is supposed to be a class about the world's religions, not about your psyches.

Thomas: Sorry, Bea. I really wasn't trying to make you feel uncomfortable, I was just trying to help you make your thoughts clearer.

Bea: Maybe there are some thoughts that *can't* be made clear. You know, there are mystics in every religion: not just Hindus and Buddhists but Christians and Jews and Muslims too.

Fesser: That's true. And we also find the opposite: in every religion where mysticism is central—in Hinduism and Buddhism, at least—there are also non-mystical options. In Hinduism there's bhakti yoga, which is more personal. They don't claim to *be* Brahman, just to love Brahman. And the same in Buddhism: the Pure Land sect believes in the reality of the personal self, both in Buddha and in us. They believe in what they call "other-power." They say Buddha is a savior who will take you to the Pure Land, or paradise, and they say you should have faith in him and love him. And in the West, where that kind of personalism is the main line, both for us and for God, all three religions also have mystics who seem to say pantheistic-sounding things. Even in Islam there are some Sufi mystics who sound like pantheists.

Thomas: So what do you conclude from that data, Professor?

Fesser: At least this much: that religions provide two paths, not just one—two different interpretations of religious experience: the personal and the impersonal, or the

personal and the mystical, or the theistic and the pantheistic. Even if both sides believe the authority of
their official scriptures, there's usually a mystical and
a non-mystical interpretation of them.

Thomas: Why do you think that happens?

Fesser: The two kinds of religions seem to be two different
psychological paradigms for two different psychological
types of people.

Thomas: Are you saying it's just "different strokes for different
folks"? So you can't identify any religion by its official
creeds or scriptures?

Fesser: No, it's not quite that relativistic. By the way, Christianity is the only religion that has *creeds*. Unless you
count the Muslim shahada as a creed: "There is no God
but God and Muhammad is his prophet."

Thomas: Professor, you're a convinced pluralist, right?

Fesser: Yes, I'm a pluralist, but pluralism doesn't mean I claim
to know the falsehood of either inclusivism or exclusivism. Perhaps I'm a pluralist about the three *philosophies*—pluralism and exclusivism and inclusivism.
Perhaps there is a truth in each of them.

Thomas: But they contradict each other.

Fesser: Perhaps. Bea would say they don't.

Thomas: But if she's wrong, I'm right. And if I'm wrong,
she's right.

Bea: Only if your either/or logic is absolute, Thomas.

Thomas: Well, it either is or it isn't. You can't avoid the logical
either/or.

Bea: Mystics can.

Thomas: They either can or they can't. So you're back in "either/
or logic" with them too.

Fesser: This philosophical debate is really interesting, Thomas, but I think you're a bit ahead of the game again. And you too, Bea. This has happened every time we've tried to understand a religion: you couldn't help moving quickly to the other question, the question of how different religions compare to each other. For instance, last week we said very little about Islam but a lot about whether it contradicted other religions. But we're supposed to survey our data first before we compare it, remember? And today we're supposed to be talking about Christianity. And to talk about something, we have to listen first.

Bea: But we just can't help asking the comparative religions question as we look at each religion.

Fesser: Yes, you can.

Thomas: How?

Fesser: You can just look straight ahead for a little while, and only after you do that first, then turn your head and look to the side.

Bea: Is that what you're trying to have us do in this course?

Fesser: Yes. That's why I'm trying to play all the roles in our little play; that's why I'm putting on more than one hat. A few weeks ago I was a Hindu, last week I was a Jew, today I'm a Christian.

Thomas: So your pluralism is just a game? You're not really a pluralist?

Fesser: No, I didn't say that either.

Thomas: But pluralism has to be either just a game or your serious belief.

Fesser: Not so.

Bea: See, Thomas, the professor doesn't always use your either/or logic either.

Fesser: No, Bea, that's not my point either. My point is simply that there's a third possibility. Pluralism can be more than a mere game and less than a firm conclusion. It can be a method of teaching, a way of wearing many religious hats so that we can fit our heads into all of them.

Thomas: So you put on the Christian hat for this morning's class lecture?

Fesser: Yes.

Thomas: I understand your method.

Fesser: Good. Then let's all try to understand Christianity in its own terms first. And to do that, let's begin where Jesus began: with Judaism, and with the historical relation between Christianity and Judaism. We can no more understand Christianity without its Jewish roots than we can understand Buddhism without its Hindu roots.

Thomas: Professor, I remember that in the class on Buddhism you called it a kind of Hindu Protestantism, a simplification. But the relation between Judaism and Christianity is the exact opposite of that, isn't it? Christianity adds to Judaism, while Buddhism subtracts from Hinduism, or simplifies Hinduism, as Protestantism simplifies Catholicism.

Fesser: In a sense, yes, but in another sense, no, because Hindus see Buddhism as one of their own yogas, but Catholics don't see Protestants as one of many forms of Catholicism. So the parallel doesn't really work.

Thomas: But you can't be both a Jew and a Christian.

Bea: Yes, you can. In fact almost all Jews who become Christians nowadays say they are not converts out of Judaism at all, but completed Jews, fulfilled Jews. And

Christians say the same thing: they believe everything in Judaism, because Jesus did.

Thomas: But isn't it the other way around with Jews and Christians? Isn't Christianity a *simplified* Judaism? Didn't Jesus do to Judaism what Luther did to Catholicism? Didn't he reduce it to its essence, the complex to the simple, the 613 laws and Ten Commandments to just "the two great commandments"?

Bea: No, he *universalized* Judaism. He didn't give us another religion, a simpler one, so that we'd have to choose between the two. He didn't tell Jews they were wrong; he said he came to fulfill Judaism—"the law and the prophets"—not to destroy it. And he told his disciples to preach it to the whole world. He was inclusive, not exclusive.

Thomas: You always keep coming back to that, don't you? But it won't work to say Jesus was inclusive, because if he included *Judaism*, then he had to be an exclusivist, because Judaism was already an *exclusivist* religion. The scriptures of the Jews said that the pagan polytheistic religions were wrong, that all the other gods were either idols or demons. That's very clear in the Jewish scriptures. So if Jesus universalized Judaism, he universalized exclusivism, not inclusivism.

Bea: He excluded pagan polytheisms, sure, but those different pagan religions already excluded each other: their gods warred against each other. But they're all pretty much dead today. All the religions of the world are monotheistic. Jesus universalized monotheism; he universalized universalism.

Thomas: No, he did just the opposite. He universalized exclusivism. You're ignoring your scriptural data. "I am the way, and the truth, and the life. No one comes to the Father except through me." That's the most exclusivistic religious claim I've ever heard.

Bea: No, Thomas, I don't think you *have* ever heard it. You misunderstand it.

Thomas: How?

Bea: You forget the rest of your New Testament data.

Thomas: What data?

Bea: He is called "the true light that enlightens *everyone*." So he must have enlightened Krishna and Buddha and Lao Tzu and Confucius too.

Thomas: Well, I guess he forgot *me*, then. Because I don't believe that.

Bea: No, he didn't forget you. He still believes in you even if you don't believe in him.

Thomas: That's very clever, but what does it mean?

Fesser: I give up! It's just impossible to get you two to focus on the religion itself instead of on all those comparisons. You want to focus on the string and ignore the pearls.

Bea: (ignoring the professor) It means, Thomas, that Jesus is inclusive of you even though you're not inclusive of him. He's an inclusivist and you're an exclusivist, and the inclusivist can include even the exclusivist.

Thomas: (also ignoring the professor) You can't do that . . .

Bea: I just did it.

Thomas: Well, yes, in a sense of course you can. *You* can take any position at all. But a position can't take any position at all. You can try to include opposites if you want, but a position can't include its opposite. *You* can say you include everything, even exclusivism; but *inclusivism* can't include exclusivism. They exclude each other. They're opposites. You contradict yourself.

Bea: "Do I contradict myself? Very well, then, I contradict myself. I am large. I contain multitudes." Walt Whitman.

Thomas: I am going to make a radical proposal to you, Bea.

Bea: No, I won't marry you, Thomas, no matter what you say.

Thomas: Not that kind of proposal, silly. I propose we try to define our terms.

Bea: I have no problem defining my terms.

Thomas: Good. Then what does it mean "to believe in Christianity"?

Bea: It means to believe in Jesus.

Thomas: Fine. But what does it mean to believe in him?

Bea: Hmm . . . that's a big question, and a vague one.

Thomas: Then let's start with a little question and a specific one. How about the claim that divides Christians and Jews: that Jesus is the Messiah, the one promised by the prophets?

Bea: Fine. Christians do believe that.

Thomas: And most Jews don't. If they did, they'd be Christians. So how do you make that out not to be a contradiction? How can "is" be the same as "isn't"? And here's a second contradiction that's even more radical than that: Christians say he's not just a man but God. No wonder the Jews got hot under the collar. If there's anything that's a line in the sand, there it is. Christians worship him. If you don't worship him, then you're not a Christian, and if you do worship him, then you're not a good Jew, you're an idolater. How do you make that out not to be a contradiction?

Bea: A Hindu would have no problem with that. Jesus was enlightened: he realized his inner divinity.

Thomas: To a Jew that has to sound even worse than Christianity. It's saying not just that this one man is God but that every man is God. Polytheism multiplied by seven billion!

Bea: No, not *gods*, God. Not polytheism, monotheism.

Thomas: Even worse! I'm not just one of many gods, I'm the one supreme God.

Bea: We're getting confused now.

Thomas: Speak for yourself, Bea. *I'm* not confused. You are. Look, let's start with facts. Here's a man who said—at least his followers said he said—that he was God incarnate—not *a* god but *the* God, and not the Hindu "blob God" but the Jewish Creator God. This claim—that the Author of the whole play stepped into his play as one of his characters—that's either true or false. And Judaism says it's false. So if Christianity is right, Judaism is wrong, and vice versa, at least about Jesus. You have to choose. And you can't choose the whole, or the all, or the blob God, or the universal. You can't choose "Here comes everybody." Because that's not a choice. You have to choose a particular. God or no God. One God or many. The snob God or the blob God. Jesus as God or Jesus as not God. There has to be a no for you to choose a yes. If yes includes no, then you can't *choose* yes, you're forced to be part of yes, even if you say no.

Bea: But Hinduism's God isn't a blob God and Judaism's God isn't a snob God, and Jesus isn't either the snob or the blob. He's got a personality, so he's not a blob. And he came all the way down to earth and evil and suffering and death, so he's not a snob. Your dilemma doesn't apply to him.

Thomas: Okay, maybe my "blob God versus snob God" isn't a good dilemma. Maybe there's a third possibility about Jesus. But there can't be any third possibility between saying that Jesus is that third possibility and saying that he isn't. Jesus is either the God he claimed to be or he isn't. And Christians say he is and everybody else says he isn't. Because if a Christian came to believe that he isn't, then he wouldn't be a Christian anymore. And if anybody else said he is, they'd become a Christian just by believing that. That's as clear a line in the sand as I ever saw in religion.

Bea: And you—what do you believe, Thomas?

Thomas: You know what I believe, Bea. I don't believe *anybody* is God, not even God!

Bea: What do you say to somebody that antireligious, Professor?

Fesser: Oh, I wouldn't say anything at all unless he asked me.

Thomas: Suppose somebody asked you?

Fesser: That depends on who it is. Not everybody deserves the same answer.

Thomas: I'm not everybody, Professor, I'm just me.

Fesser: All right, Thomas, since you asked, here is my answer. I think your apparently clear and simple logic is landing you in waters that are to you more threatening, more uncomfortable, more deep, dark, and dangerous than you think.

Thomas: Why do you call it dangerous? I'm agnostic. That's the opposite of dangerous. That's playing it safe, not fighting on either side. I say neither yea nor nay, even though I think it's more likely that it's nay. What's dangerous about that line of thinking?

Fesser: It's getting close to two arguments for Christianity that I think you want to avoid. One of them is the "liar, lunatic, or Lord" argument and the other one is Pascal's wager.

Thomas: I'm familiar with both arguments. Why do you call them dangerous?

Fesser: Because of their either/or logic.

Thomas: I still don't see the danger.

Fesser: Tell me, when you have a religious either/or, which do you think is easier to do, to refute one side or to prove the other?

Thomas: To refute, of course.

Fesser: Then apply that to these two either/or arguments for Christianity—the Lord, liar, or lunatic argument and Pascal's wager. They don't directly and positively try to prove their religious conclusion, like the first cause argument or the design argument or the moral argument. They just refute an "either." And either/or logic then lands you smack dab in the middle of the "or." So it's really only Bea's both/and logic that protects your agnosticism. Either/or logic makes you choose. If you don't make the wager, you risk hell. If you don't say Jesus is Lord, you have to say he's a liar or a lunatic, not a great religious teacher, because he claimed to be the Lord. There's risk either way.

Thomas: But I avoid both dogmatic atheism and dogmatic theism by avoiding dogmatism. I don't wager either way. I just watch the game. I'm an agnostic, remember, not a dogmatic atheist.

Fesser: But can you do that? If you're already "embarked," as Pascal puts it, embarked on human life in time, then you can't just be a kind of timeless, objective,

	impersonal observer. You're involved, not detached.
	Even your choice to be detached involves you in a choice.
Thomas:	Are you trying to argue me into religion?
Fesser:	No. In fact I'm almost doing the opposite: warning you
	about it. I'm not telling you what to do, but I'm advising
	you to look carefully at what lies ahead in the road
	when you put your high-beam headlights on. I per-
	sonally sympathize with your desire to avoid dog-
	matism, Thomas. But suppose you have to make a leap
	of faith one way or the other without any dogmatic
	assurances?
Thomas:	Why should I suppose that?
Fesser:	Because you're embarked on the ship called life.
Thomas:	Of course I'm alive. Therefore what?
Fesser:	Therefore you're going to die. That's life's one certainty.
	And at that point the wager clicks in one way or the
	other. Either you meet God or not. And if you do, it's
	either heaven or hell. That's what Pascal the existen-
	tialist would say, anyway.
Thomas:	Oh.
Bea:	Why do you look so shocked, Thomas? Isn't that either/
	or right up your alley? That's exclusivism.
Thomas:	Because it's not just a logical exclusivism but an
	existential one.
Bea:	You look like you just met a ghost.
Fesser:	Mind you, I'm not trying to sway your mind in any
	way. I'm just throwing out what I think Pascal would say.
Thomas:	Why?
Fesser:	To see what you make of it.
Thomas:	I . . . I don't know *what* to make of it. I'll have to think
	about that.

Fesser: That's why I threw it out. I'm not in the business of pushing anybody to make the leap of faith. *Any* leap of faith, pro or con. I'm just in the business of making them think about it in every possible way. That's what the course is about.

Thomas: Thanks, Professor. I appreciate that.

Fesser: And you, Bea: how come you seem even more discombobulated than Thomas?

Bea: I don't know. I guess I'll have to do some more thinking too.

Fesser: What are you thinking right now that you weren't thinking before?

Bea: Frankly, I'm thinking that maybe my inclusivism isn't as safe as I thought it was either. Maybe I'm trying to avoid the wager even more than Thomas is.

Fesser: Wow. Two As in one day for the professor! And I thought today's class was a failure.

COMPARATIVE RELIGIONS
Can Contradictories Both Be True?

Fesser: Hi, guys. What do you want to talk about today? (*As if he didn't know.*)

Bea: Today's class, please. Because we finally got to the bottom line of the course. I want to find the truth about how religions compare.

Fesser: What did you think about what we said in today's class about that question?

Bea: I found it fascinating, but it made me more confused than ever.

Fesser: And do you think that's a bad thing?

Bea: I see your point, Professor. Confusion makes us think. So it's good for us. But it doesn't feel very good.

Fesser: What about you, Thomas? Did it make you more confused too?

Thomas: No, I had the opposite reaction: I thought it was very clarifying.

Fesser: How?

Thomas: I think I can explain that by connecting it with the very first class, the one where we tried to define religion and failed, because all our definitions were either too broad or too narrow. And that was because we were trying to define two very different things in the same definition: Western religions and Eastern religions. Well, I think we have the same problem in comparing different religions and asking whether they're inclusive or exclusive: we're trying to compare apples and oranges.

Fesser: Okay, but why didn't you find that confusing? We found some Eastern-style mystics and apparent pantheists appearing in all three Western religions, and we found examples of Western-style religion—personal and theistic—appearing in Hinduism and Buddhism too. It's like finding yin at the heart of yang and yang at the heart of yin.

Thomas: Yes.

Fesser: Tell me, why didn't you find that confusing?

Bea: *I* certainly did.

Thomas: Because what that shows is just how theistic and pantheistic options appear within each religion. It shows why we couldn't find a "one size fits all" definition for both of those kinds of religions during that first class.

Fesser: And did you come to understand inclusivism better from this course, Thomas?

Thomas: Yes.

Fesser: How?

Thomas: I came to see that Eastern religions are inclusive in *three* ways. First, they include a Western-style option. Second, they can include each other: it's possible to be both a Hindu and a Buddhist, or a Taoist and a

Confucian, as it's *not* possible to be both a Christian and a Muslim or a Christian and a Jew. Third, they're inclusivist about salvation; they don't have an eternal hell.

Fesser: That third point is a different kind of inclusivism: not about truth but about salvation.

Thomas: Okay, you clarified that for me. Thanks.

Fesser: What else did you find clarifying, Thomas?

Thomas: About the truth question, you mean, as distinct from the salvation question?

Fesser: Yes, since that seems to be your specialty.

Thomas: Your point about there being not only three philosophies about comparing religions—exclusivism, inclusivism, and pluralism—but also three philosophies about comparing these three philosophies. An exclusivist would say that the three philosophies are as exclusive of each other as the different religions are: that if one is true, then the other two are false. An inclusivist would say that they include each other and that they're all true, just as all religions include each other and they're all true. And a pluralist would say that the three philosophies can't be compared any more than the different religions can be compared, they're just different.

Bea: You found that clarifying? I found it confusing.

Thomas: That's because you don't like to think logically, Bea. But I have one problem with that, Professor. Maybe it's not clear whether *religions* logically exclude each other or not, because religions aren't merely rational things. But whether these three *philosophies* exclude each other or not has to be clear, because philosophies appeal only to reason. So I don't see how you can possibly be a pluralist about the three philosophies, although I do see how you can be a pluralist about the different religions.

Fesser: Have all the philosophical problems in the history of philosophy been clearly solved, Thomas?

Thomas: Of course not.

Fesser: Then you shouldn't expect that philosophy is going to be a whole lot simpler and clearer than religion, even though it appeals to reason alone, right?

Thomas: I guess so.

Fesser: Then not claiming to have solved the exclusivism-versus-inclusivism problem is not irresponsible or un-reasonable. I see strong arguments for both positions, and so I can't simply say one of them has refuted the other.

Thomas: Okay, that's reasonable. That's like my agnosticism. I understand that. But I still don't understand how an inclusivism about the three *philosophies* can possibly be true, even though I do understand how someone like Bea can believe in an inclusivism of *religions*. Let's assume you buy the diver analogy, inclusivism being like a diver going deep and seeing all the islands as one landmass underwater. I don't believe that, but I think I understand how somebody can believe it. What I don't understand is how anyone can believe that about the three philosophies. The inclusivist says that inclusivism includes exclusivism. How can that be? It's not logical.

Bea: Because philosophy is more than logic, Thomas.

Thomas: You're saying philosophy is something like religious mysticism?

Bea: Yes.

Thomas: How?

Bea: Philosophy can see things from a deeper point of view too, just as religious mysticism can. You've never opened your third eye, Thomas, the eye of the heart, the intuitive eye. All you know is the eyes of your body and the eyes of your brain.

Thomas: But I explain all the data with those two eyes. It's just a different explanation than yours.

Bea: No, you don't. You can't account for the mystics and for their agreement across the borders of religions.

Thomas: I can account for the mystics very easily. Mystical experience is a trick of the brain, a hallucination, an illusion. But you can't call logic an illusion.

Bea: Oh yes, I can.

Fesser: I have a suggestion for both of you. From the beginning of this course you've both been arguing continually and getting nowhere. Don't you draw any conclusion from *that* datum, from your failure to convince each other?

Thomas: Professor, I think you're drawing a different conclusion from that than we are. Because my conclusion is that Bea just refuses to use the logical part of her brain, and her conclusion is that I refuse to use the illogical part of my brain. But you've not favored either one of us so far, and I suspect you're not going to do that today either. So what's your conclusion? What's your explanation of our standoff?

Fesser: When there's a standoff, there's often a common mistake parties are making.

Bea: I see what it is! It's the assumption that we can't both be right.

Fesser: No, that's *your* diagnosis of the problem, Bea, but it's not Thomas's.

Bea: But what's yours?

Fesser: That you're both rushing to judgment. You're getting nowhere because you insist on being judgmental toward each other before listening and learning from each other, as we were supposed to be listening and learning from each religion. You see, I'm arguing for a most humble position. That's what pluralism is. It focuses on the facts, on the details. Because "God is in the details." In the empirical facts, in what we can see. We need to look long and hard before we argue. That's what I find very useful about the method called phenomenology.

Thomas: Okay, let's look at the facts, or the details, or the phenomena, if you think that will help us. What details do you think would help us resolve our standoff?

Fesser: Well, how about the three dimensions of every religion that we found the first week? Remember? When we failed to find a single *definition* of religion, when we didn't define its single essence, we did find a single *description* of it when we were satisfied just to describe its three appearances. Every religion has a creed, a code, and a cult; or words, works, and worship. Remember?

Thomas: Okay. So what?

Fesser: Creeds contradict each other, don't they? Isn't that their purpose? To define heresies?

Thomas: Yes.

Fesser: So exclusivism seems true in that dimension. And moral codes—the moral codes of all the world's religions are not just similar but strikingly similar. They all want to uproot the master instinct of selfishness. That's a very profound inclusivism and agreement, isn't it?

Bea: Yes.

Fesser: And each religion has within it many different methods or modes of worship, whether it's liturgies or prayers or paths to mystical experience or yoga methods. So pluralism is true there, not just between different religions but even within every religion.

Bea: Right.

Fesser: So each of the three philosophies of comparative religion has some truth, each about a different dimension of religion. So maybe for them to argue about who's right is like the three blind men arguing about whether an elephant is a tree, a wall, or a snake. They're all right. One felt his leg, one felt his side, one felt his trunk.

Thomas: Fine. You don't deny that analogy, and I don't deny it, but Bea denies it.

Bea: No I don't. That's a favorite image of the inclusivists! Why do you say I deny it?

Thomas: Look at the data of those three phenomenological dimensions, as the professor says. There's no "comparative religions problem" with codes or cults, only creeds. That's where all the problems are, all the contradictions between religions, right?

Bea: Yes.

Thomas: And you deny the exclusivism of those contradictions. But we exclusivists don't deny the inclusivism of codes, or the pluralism of cults. I don't deny your part of the elephant, but you deny mine. I don't deny your data, you deny mine.

Bea: No, you deny my data too, because my data for inclusivism is not just the oneness of moral codes but also the oneness of mystical experience.

Thomas: I don't deny it, I explain it. It's an illusion.

Bea: So it's that simple? Saint John of the Cross and Buddha and Lao Tzu and Shankara are all just fools?

Thomas: No, not fools. Deep dreamers. I'm not saying I'm smarter than they are. I might be suckered into believing it too if I had those dreams. But mystical experiences can be wrong. They're not infallible.

Bea: What *can't* be wrong?

Thomas: The law of non-contradiction. Which is why I can't believe your mystics. They deny the one most certain thing, the one and only totally undeniable thing, without which nothing makes any sense at all, including the denial of it. You just *can't* deny it.

Bea: I do deny it!

Thomas: If you do deny it, then you don't deny it. Because if you do deny it, if you deny the law of non-contradiction, then you deny that anything contradicts anything; and that means you deny that denying it contradicts *not* denying it.

Bea: Thomas, you are making my head spin.

Thomas: Thank you for the compliment.

Bea: It's not a compliment. It's spinning in the wrong direction.

Thomas: And therefore it's spinning in the right direction, if there's no contradiction between right and wrong. You can't do it, Bea, you just can't pull it off. Quarrelling with the law of non-contradiction is like intellectual suicide. Your gun is shooting yourself, not me.

Fesser: I think Thomas has a valid point, Bea, even though I'm as sympathetic to the claims of mysticism as you are, and I don't dismiss them as illusions, as Thomas does. But he certainly has a point about creeds, and propositions, and words, even if his point may not be valid outside of creeds and words and propositions.

Bea: Then let's overcome creeds and words and propositions. We have to have more than words and propositions if we're going to have any religion at all. Thomas wants to just ignore mystical experiences. He's ignoring the data.

Fesser: Well, of course we have to have more than words and propositions. And of course we should not ignore mystical experiences. But when we speak, we can't—we literally can't—ignore the laws of logic either. You look unconvinced. Let me tell you a little story to show you how even we defenders of mysticism can't ignore the laws of logic, okay?

Bea: Okay.

Fesser: There was a Hindu thinker who converted to Christianity and became a Christian philosopher and theologian. His name is Ravi Zacharias. He tells this story. He was lecturing about Christianity at Harvard, and one of his Hindu friends whom he had known in India was in the audience. Afterward they met, as old friends, and went to a Chinese restaurant together, just the two of them. They sat on opposite sides of a table in a booth. His friend said to Ravi, "Ravi, I'm happy for you that you have found your yoga, your religious way. I have no quarrel with you for being a Christian. But you seem to have a quarrel with me for being a Hindu. Because in your speech you tried to argue that everyone should believe in Christianity, because your guru, Jesus, is the *only* way. That's narrow, Ravi. That's either/or

logic. You haven't progressed, Ravi, you've regressed.
You don't need to give up Hinduism to embrace Christianity; Hinduism includes everything. I include you,
but you don't include me. My both/and Hindu logic
affirms and includes even your Christian either/or logic,
but you won't do the same to me. Why did you become
so narrow minded?"

And Ravi replied, "Let me see if I understand you.
You're saying that I made a mistake in leaving Hinduism
to become a Christian, and leaving your both/and inclusivism to embrace an either/or exclusivism, right?"

"Right," the friend said.

"So I should go back to your both/and logic, your
Hindu inclusivism. Because either/or is a mistake."

"Right."

"So you're saying that I'm sitting on the wrong side
of this table right now, the either/or side, the side that
says there are two different sides of the table; and
you're sitting on the right side of the table, the both/
and side, the side that says there aren't really two different sides of the table."

At that, his friend, who was quite bright, saw the
point and said, "Oh, dear, that nasty old law of non-
contradiction never seems to go away, does it?"

Bea: Are you arguing for Christianity over Hinduism, then,
professor? Or for exclusivism over inclusivism?
Or what?

Fesser: Neither. I'm just arguing for not ignoring the *problem*
in inclusivism.

Bea: Oh. I see. You're saying that I can't ignore logic any
more than Ravi's friend could.

Fesser: Exactly. Not just that you *shouldn't*, but that you *can't*.

Thomas: And do you see an equally serious problem in exclusivism, Professor?

Fesser: Yes, I think I do.

Thomas: What is it?

Fesser: Did you ever hear the cliché, "Don't knock it until you try it"?

Thomas: Yeah. That's what a drug dealer says when he's trying to hook you on a drug.

Fesser: It's also what Juliet's sister said to Romeo to persuade him to try a date with Juliet. And what a mother says to her little baby who screws up his face at ice cream. You're assuming that mystical experience is deceptive, like drugs. *How do you know* those mystical divers don't see something that's true down there where the water's too deep for ordinary light?

Thomas: I don't.

Fesser: And Bea, how do you *know* they do?

Bea: I don't.

Fesser: And so we end where Socrates began: with the knowledge that we don't really know. Thank you both for being so open and so honest. You're very good students, both of you.

POSTSCRIPT

I will make this very short. I think I have already said too much about exclusivism, inclusivism, and pluralism. To quote the *Tao Te Ching*, "Knowing that enough is enough—is enough."

OTHER BOOKS
BY PETER KREEFT